Art and War

Art and War

Poetry,
Pulp and Politics
in Israeli Fiction

Lavie Tidhar
Shimon Adaf

Published by Repeater Books
An imprint of Watkins Media Ltd
19-21 Cecil Court
London
WC2N 4EZ
UK

www.repeaterbooks.com
A Repeater Books paperback original 2016
1

Distributed in the United States by Random House, Inc., New York.

ISBN: 978-1-910924-04-4
Ebook ISBN: 978-1-910924-05-1

Cover design: Johnny Bull
Typography and typesetting: Jan Middendorp
Typefaces: Chaparral Pro and Vito
Printed and bound in Great Britain

Introduction

I first met Shimon Adaf five years ago, though I seem to recall seeing him, once, years before, when he was the bright young fiction editor for Keter Publishing – the youngest editor ever to assume that position. He was not yet, then, Adaf the prize-winning poet and novelist, and I do not think that we were introduced.

In early 2010 I returned to live in Israel for a time. It so happened that I was asked to appear on a literary panel alongside Shimon – the subject was, if I remember rightly, future visions of the Middle East, or something to that effect. I enjoyed arguing with him, and we continued the conversation in the nearby cafeteria, where it transpired that, though neither of us had read the other's work, it so happened that we lived a mere five minute walk apart from each other, in Jaffa.

We agreed to do what writers are wont to do, which was to meet up and exchange books – the one thing writers are *not* poor in. It didn't take me long to become a huge fan of this quietly spoken, fiercely intelligent writer, whose *Sunburnt Faces* kept me up reading all through the night, and whose novel *Kfor* seemed to me a genuine revelation, a staggering literary achievement that became an influence on my own future work.

For the next year we'd meet up every so often in one of the bars or cafés near the vast flea market in Jaffa, where we continued carrying on our conversation: about books, writing, politics...

Shimon and I grew up on opposite sides of the Israeli spectrum. I grew up in the north, on a kibbutz – a sort of Zionist, socialist commune – while Shimon grew up in the south, in Sderot, a poor town in the desert just five kilometres from Gaza, the son of religious parents who had emigrated from Morocco. My own family had come from Europe, one half Zionist idealists, one half Holocaust survivors. Shimon was destined to live the life of a great rabbi – I was destined to become a farmer or a soldier, I suspect, though I would have made a poor job of either.

Instead, I went travelling (and never quite stopped) while Shimon became a budding musician in Tel Aviv. And yet, though our experiences growing up couldn't have been more different, they were more similar than not in many ways, and shared one abiding passion – the translated American science fiction that was available to us at the time. As youthful readers, we devoured them all. As adults, we were both drawn to the same writers who utilised literature in strange and unsettling new ways.

In due course, I moved back to London, though Shimon and I continued to correspond by e-mail, and chat on Skype (those science fictional tools we always knew will be waiting for us in the future!). At some point I was able to help secure a small hardcover publication of *Sunburnt Faces* in its English translation (Shimon's first novel to be published in English, but only, I hope, the first of many), and saw it launched in England in 2013, alongside my own *The Violent Century*. In preparation for that, I decided to interview Shimon, but the interview soon became another conversation, eventually published as *The Convergence Between Poetry and the Fantastic*.

At that point, I think, the idea for this book was firmly planted, in my mind at least. During the summer of 2014, we

7

attempted to carry on the conversation as events in Israel took a violent turn. Both of us, I think, were too depressed then to continue; instead, we each wrote a short story (they are included here), which together constituted their own kind of dialogue.

A year later, we felt more ready to carry on, and this book is, finally, the result. I hope it will be of interest.

Lavie Tidhar
2015

PART ONE

Art and War

Lavie

I've been thinking a lot recently about what we mean by a 'writing career' or, more precisely, the arc of writing, the sort of meta-narrative that's made up of the gradual progression of everything you write. For instance, it seems to me that a lot of writers do their most ambitious, honest work early on. As though we have that one great burst that's then followed by drudgery, by routine. Heller with *Catch-22* is a good example. One thing that struck me, a sort of motivation, is the idea of what happens if you die before writing that one book you should have written but didn't. There was a writer who died recently of cancer. He was known for his cancer – he documented it, very movingly – but what kept me awake at night was the thought that he never wrote the book his early promise might have suggested he would. And I can't honestly say why: he was a prolific short story writer, who then went on to have a string of novels out and they were, well, sort of mediocre. And then he died. And it's really bothered me, that maybe you have that thought, I'll just write for now for the money, and then I'll be able to write that real book later on, but that later on never comes. The thought that you could get hit by a bus tomorrow, or get cancer, and have nothing to show for it.

I guess it's partly why I've resisted the easy path, in a way. *Osama* was the book I believed in, but no one was willing to publish it for a long time. *A Man Lies Dreaming* sounded like a bad joke – it feels like a miracle to me that it came out, and I wasn't sure it would until three months before the publication date!

But at least I can say: I've written those books, I've done a handful of short stories I think are as good as anything out there – if I get hit by a bus tomorrow I can diet with a clean conscience.

But I've been struggling a lot with following up on *A Man Lies Dreaming*. It's the one book I'm really happy with, and I just – how do you follow something like that? It's not like I really know how I wrote it. I wish I did! I thought writing should get easier the more you do it, but it just seems to me to get harder. And I was struck by something, a line in the film *Infamous*, about Truman Capote. And Capote couldn't write anymore after *In Cold Blood*. Sandra Bullock plays Harper Lee, and Lee is interviewed for the camera and she says something like, "Well, sometimes that's all there is".

That really stuck with me. And Lee, of course, never finished another book after *To Kill A Mockingbird*. I mean, how do you possibly follow that? And she talks, in the movie, about this idea that writers have to keep producing, keep writing, but why exactly is that? I often think of Philip Larkin, too, who, about three years before his death, woke up and said, "There isn't anymore". The poetry was just gone.

(This was written before *Go, Set A Watchman* was published in July 2015, yet the statement remains true: *Watchman* is the earlier novel, the draft from which *Mockingbird* later emerged.)

So this worries me. I think about it a lot. It's harder for me to write. And I keep wondering if it's worth it. Do I have anything left to say? Can I rediscover my anger? I think I'm motivated by anger, more than anything. Though I can't imagine running out of things to be angry about!

But what I wanted to ask you, is about your own 'career progression'. Your first novel, *Two Days and a Mile Before Sunset*, is quite accessible. It's got flashes of the weirdness that I'd argue characterises your later work, but it's essentially a literary, contemporary detective novel. It's about the music scene in 90s Tel Aviv. It's very relatable for an Israeli reader. And your third novel, *Sunburnt Faces* – I remember reading it almost in one go. It has more of the weirdness in it, but it's a very smooth read. Whereas my feeling is that in your latest works, *Undercities* and *The Wedding Gifts*, you demand a lot from the reader. You've stopped making *allowances*. I feel – I could be very wrong! – that you're writing more for yourself than for some idea of a reader. It's almost as though you've become more selfish. I find them much harder to read. They're even denser – and your work has always been dense!

And it's an interesting question to me, too, because what we do, after all, is write to be published. Writing as a form of communication. And for me, I know it's a struggle to balance what I want with what the hypothetical reader – who might be you (since you've very graciously been looking at some of my early drafts), who might be my agent, might be some random person in a library somewhere – wants. You could argue that writing is the art of compromise. And I get the sense you're tired of compromising.

Shimon

In recent years, I got fed up with stories, plots, narrative devices. The reason verges on the metaphysical, I think, and therefore must have some kernel of truth to it. I am a reader. Some of the most intense experiences of early age, I had through reading. Voices came out of the book and they were there only for me. I didn't assume that they were meant for other readers as well. I was their sole listener. Of course, none of this stayed for long. I guess every childhood stage is a small psychosis in its own right. But I long for this kind of intimacy. Deep within a book (and a lot of time while reading Jewish scriptures, mainly the Talmud), I feel its lure: a stroke of homesickness, a promise of connectivity, a fleeting sense of a meaningful way of being.

Is this the situation I'm trying to recreate as a writer – to be a voice in someone else's mind for a short while? I guess it is. The problem with that is that you cannot calculate the means to achieve it, you cannot fathom them. The measures involved are so random, so fickle. We are talking about the unexplorable land that is the very domain and nature of literature itself: other people. (Poe was fundamentally wrong about this, maybe the only instance in which he was wrong: it's impossible to have the focus of the work in the effect on others, and still be able to plan it.)

So, starting to write fiction, I turned to the devices at hand – manufacturing narratives by using forms and structures I knew from reading. I was trying to contain, so to speak, the experience I wished to express, in pre-made containers – stories and tropes, as if they could pass on the emotional and intellectual content, deliver it safely. But the result always filled me with unease. I wasn't content. I felt I was compromising. And then something awful, unbearable happened to me. I lost someone, and the loss made me realise that it's never the story that carries emotion and experience for me, but language. It's simple really: loss teaches violence. In demonstrating the limits of language in giving life, it proves how language is indispensable in achieving the knowledge of being alive – you have to smash your spirit against these limits, you have to learn to use the broken body anew. My first works were poetry, and I never abandoned poetry as way of dealing with being. Nothing is real for me unless it is expressed in the right way of using language. That's what ignites the sense of intimacy, and yet, saying so, I could not get to back to poetry in its purest phase. The echo chamber of the story is still needed, but not the story itself. I came to detest stories, yet I find myself immersed in them, both as a reader and a writer. That's my struggle – I don't think about what a hypothetical or a real reader would want, but how to offer to some unknown other what ails me, in the best manner in my power.

Now, I know that it is an important aspect of your writing – serving as a reader of others' works, making tributes and using tropes and popular genres. Since the first work by you that I read, in Hebrew, I got the feeling that your work is in the making, especially in the novels – you know the starting point, which is an idea or a prevalent concept in fiction or culture, and you construct a plot in order to investigate it. Why is it that you are so interested in genres and popular culture, and yet all the while you are trying to escape them through reflection, through criticism? You raised many questions in your previous passage, yet I feel the relationship with the audience is the pivotal one, from which all the other issues stem. Why can't you write a novel that is completely oblivious either to popular forms or to your need to reflect on them?

Lavie

My first response to this question was: fear. Thinking about it, though, I'm not sure how honest it is as an answer. The fear element comes from my own sense of doubt. I often say it – I'd like to think I'm a literary writer playing in genre, but I think the truth is I'm essentially a pulp writer with aspirations. I love stories – but at the same time, I think I overgorged on them, I had too many too quickly, and now, like eating too much candyfloss in one night, I don't like them so much. (And yet look at me. I can't help it with the similes. It's got to the point even my wife's making fun of me about them.

Though I really did once sell candyfloss, and ate so much of it I couldn't stomach it again for a year. Write what you know, and so on.)

What interests me is artifice. The sort of writing – genre writing, I suppose we'd say – that seeks to engulf you in the work, that seeks to make you forget you're reading a construct – I used to love that but now I just find it dishonest. Yet at the same time, I have to have story, and I'm drawn to the bizarre, to the outrageous. I think a lot of writing that is maybe beautiful writing can feel very empty. Words shouldn't be there to be pretty. They should serve something more.

I like genres because I like formula. And I like formula because essentially I like structure. I have no interest in writing a formula story for the story's sake, only in what I can do with it. To me a plot is essentially meaningless. I am not interested in plots. So I can pick one off the shelf, so to speak – a quest for something, say – and that allows me to discard the need for it. It gives me a skeleton, a shape. I don't usually plan ahead – though I'm changing, I'm planning more and more and writing less and less these days – but to me the joy in the writing is in finding out what happens next. Formula is constraint, and art needs constraint. Look at Oulipo, and the strange constraints they kept trying to use. I don't claim any kinship with Oulipo, but the constraint of formula is very liberating for me. It frees me to do other things.

But then the fear sets in again. Do I create elaborate explanations to justify, essentially, being a hack writer? I could probably make a comfortable living writing a series of detective novels, or a series of epic fantasy novels, or anything else you can think of. But it would bore me. What I try to do is come at big topics from a skewed angle. The Holocaust as pulp. Israel and Palestine viewed through alternate history.

I'm fascinated by alternate histories. Terrorism as a detective novel, in *Osama*. I suppose I am trying to do the best I can with the tools I have. I am finding it harder to find the anger that I need in order to write, though.

You're right that I have a very ambivalent relationship with my hypothetical readership. Who, in God's name, am I writing for? I abandoned Hebrew for English, very consciously, reasoning I'd rather be a small fish in a big pond, etc., etc. – and it's telling that none of my novels are published in Israel, for instance. We just can't sell them there at all. So who am I writing for? Parts of my life are completely alien to non-Israelis. I grew up on a kibbutz. I started explaining communal sleeping to a friend once, and she reacted in horror! (I still want to write that kibbutz novel. It would be a Western.) But parts of my thinking are completely alien to Israelis, too. I am neither of one party nor the other. And I fear my characters reflect that too much – they are indecisive, a bit alienated, they *drift*. Joe in *Osama* is me, essentially. He's just a drifter who never grew up. So there's something juvenile about what I do, what writers do, really, which is make stuff up.

But then, grownups can be so boring!

And this is something that fascinates me about you. If I could pinpoint one obsession you have, it's with adolescence. That is at the core of your writing. It permeates every book you write. What is it about adolescence that you can't let go of? What is the overwhelming fascination?

Shimon

Sometimes I get the feeling I never survived my coming of age. In other times, it seems to me an alien notion, considering adolescence as a calamity. I tried to address it in one of my novels, *Sunburnt Faces*, in which the heroine, Ory Elhayani, is having a divine revelation at the age of twelve, and for her, religious experience becomes synonymous with the very essence of childhood, with the concept of Wonderland, with passing into a magical reality in which all the horrors of adult life are suspended, the horrors of consciousness – the consciousness of death, the consciousness of sex, the consciousness of language, being an arbitrary tool that capture your own emotions, the world outside of you.

For her these are moments of becoming a devoted reader, and as a result, of becoming a person for whom life is shaped by literature. So the literary experience is connected with being called by an outer authority, and is both the cause of the change, and what protects her from its consequences. Language is both sacred and threatening.

Here I must protest – you present a false dichotomy concerning words. Why is it that we find instances of language pretty to begin it? No, not pretty. I never considered words to be pretty, but infused with beauty and awe, and always in texts, in the context of literary intension. Words are ominously beautiful because they carry with them echoes from the times we could surrender to the feeling that language did capture a deeper sense of reality.

For me, then, literature is the most pleasurable trap of all, I think. And I'm struck every time anew by the ingenuity of the trapping mechanism. I have this small hope that by studying it I'll be able to escape. It's a fool's hope, I know, but I keep trying to decipher it, first by turning to the years I first became aware of it, when it sprung into being. So many of my novels are compulsively origin stories, a study in the birth of awareness.

It is a strange thing, though. I don't fully accept the psychoanalytical premise of modern times, the belief that getting to know your biography or finding out the major events of your life, when you knew intense pleasure or were hurt, scarred, can serve as keys to your personality, your private patterns of addictions and ticks. Yet, I can't avoid the urge to explore the childhood of my characters. I can't grasp them, write about them, before I manage to figure them out, for myself, as children. I don't have the romantic concept of childhood to blame: that children are nature embodied, that they are pure, the closest to an authentic existence, that the birth of awareness is some sort of a corruption. It's too Christian a notion for me. I think it has more to do with viewing childhood as a period impregnated with the possible, in which the speculative is the actual. I want to see them when they didn't hope or despair, but lived the 'could-have-been' as reality.

This is not foreign to you. Stories for you are the playground of speculation, and you claim that words have to serve a purpose. But you started out by writing poetry and you come back to writing it through your recurrent protagonist Lior Tirosh. Does poetry allow you the freedom from the need of language to be functional, of the form of stories? What does poetry do for you?

Lavie

But you're the one now presenting a false dichotomy! You seem to suggest poetry has no purpose beyond itself. But of course, poetry is not at all – or not just, at any rate – about the words. It's what you do with them. The words are shaped to suit the purpose. And I think poetry is to language like an encryption or compression algorithm, only better. A poem should express multiple things with as few words as possible. A novel's a massive thing. It sprawls. It goes here and there and everywhere. It can stop for a picnic. A poem can't do that.

And I think that's my tragedy, that I am a decent enough poet, but I'm not a *great* poet. I can only see so far, and no farther. I'm a novelist by defeat. Though I'm not sure I'm even a novelist. Novels are essentially alien to me. I don't understand them – so much stuff needs to happen in novels. All those words. I think I find myself most comfortable in short stories, which I write far too many of, probably. Whereas you, I recall, don't feel the same way. You like to write big, long novels. And there's a sort of paradox there, isn't there? Between the compactness of poetry and the expansiveness of novels?

My first – and so far only – poetry collection was written when I was young. When I discovered poetry. I simply never realised you could *do* that with words. And when I suddenly realised it, it was amazing. I was about 17, I think. And I became obsessed with writing poems, not for publication or any other goal – just for the sheer joy of it. That's something I've mostly lost, I think, but that I can sometimes find in fiction now. My early poems – the stuff in the collection – were mostly written during my travelling. Early morning in a train station in Bulgaria, sick with malaria on the shores of Lake Malawi, hitchhiking in Mozambique... and I remember – I never told you this – when I was looking for a publisher, I sent the poems to Natan Yonatan, the poet (my mother knew him). He was editing a prestigious poetry line at the time. And he returned them quite perfunctorily! He said they were "merely a travel journal".

And – wounded pride aside! – I thought then, and I think now, that that's nonsense. To me, the one thing that distinguishes poetry from fiction, to an extent, is honesty. A poem must be honest. It must go into the very core of who you are, to have an emotional honesty (fiction needs it too of course, but it can function without it. Poetry can't). And it reflects who you are, where you are. My life has been lived on the road to a large extent. I have been to places, and seen things, few people can claim to have done. Certainly not Natan Yonatan! And part of my 'job', as it were, is to record moments. That's all a poem is. The record of a moment, that has never been before and will never be again. Moments from my childhood on the kibbutz, sure, but also moments from a sunset over Lake Malawi, or recovering from yet another, bad bout of malaria on Zanzibar, or shopping in a vast 24 hour supermarket in London. So, yes, in a way I think he was right. They *were* a travel journal, they just weren't *just* a travel journal.

But they were very undisciplined. Joyous. I wrote in Hebrew then. After the book came out, I didn't write poetry again for about four years. I can't write poetry like prose. Prose is like a job. You just get on with it. With poetry, I get rare bouts when I *need* to do it. When I can't stop. But I never know, when it's over, whether it will ever come back again. That intensity, that need.

When I started again, I wrote in English. I abandoned Hebrew. And I decided to write very small. To try and find that one perfect poem. That's all I ever wanted. I think of Dan Pagis' "Written in Pencil in the Sealed Railway Car". Six lines. Six! But they're perfect, it's perfect. How do you *do* that? Poems like Larkin's "Aubade". I could never write that.

So I published, a little. In a handful of British poetry magazines. But I never bothered much with publishing them. Sometimes I'd write them into my stories or the books (my editor now usually makes me take them out!). So then, Lior Tirosh, my alter-ego. The poor guy who started off by being a poet and became an obscure sci-fi writer. One version of Tirosh is the hero of one of the two novels I'm working on right now, the one that is about alternate versions of Israel.

But my point is that poems matter. They have purpose. To make us see, *feel*, something new. Something extraordinary. Of course, like novelists, most poets are pretty bad, and you end up with a lot of bland stuff about nothing. But that's in everything.

But I think, I'm not going to let you off so easy. We were talking about childhood, and I understand you when you say you don't know why you have that obsession – and also, you do go some way to explaining it in your answer, to be fair. It occurs to me childhoods for *us* – for this age we live in – are very strange because they become obsolete so quickly. Two, three hundred years ago, your child would have had the same childhood as you. The same experiences, the same place, everything replicated through the ages. For us, our childhoods come with in-built, instant nostalgia. Everything we knew, that we thought was forever, was alien to our parents, and is equally alien to people born just a few years later. I think about it a lot, in the context of my parents. In a way, I think they still live in a version of reality that hasn't been in existence in years. The "Beautiful Israel" that even as I was growing up seemed to me a construct, a stage set, that maybe never even existed. Music, expressions, ways of thinking that are all part of a past more foreign to me now than, say, the islands of Melanesia where I lived (and which actually reminded me, strongly, of my early life on the kibbutz).

You know, in English, we talk about education, which to me sounds like a practical sort of thing, an acquisition of knowledge. But in Israel, we talk about *chinuch*, which is the 'transmission of values'. And I have always been very suspicious of that, even as a child. I did not trust their values. I needed to formulate my own.

And I know we had very different upbringings, but seeing as your own adolescence, in one fictional form or another, is something you keep interrogating (in *Sunburnt Faces*, in *Mox Nox*, in *The Buried Heart*), I wonder how you yourself saw it? And how do you see it today?

Shimon

No, no, no. I didn't say that a poem is a goal unto itself, or that in poetry language is independent of the world. But that in poetry, the representational aspect of language is not its main function, that in poetry a deeper nature of words is revealed: their power to reconstruct in consciousness the bewilderment of being, and how words themselves are never enough to convey it, never enough to express the important things. In a way, for me, words – through their sonic, material presence – can transcend meaning. I can't accept poetry as an elaborate algorithm, or a complex puzzle, that the process of deciphering or rebuilding it accounts for the meaning achieved. No way. The event of meaning is far greater than the sum of meanings, context and implications.

In my novel *Undercities*, there's Akko Asido, a young computer wizard, whose sister is a poet. He truly believes that poetry is just a condensed instance of language, so he constructs algorithms to produce poetry (which leads him to a bitter fight with his sister). But it's a weird thing, the machine that he uses is never a real addressee of poetry. I'm haunted by this issue – is literature an activity that is uniquely human? Would an A.I. ever be in need of literature? Can we fathom an intelligence that has no need for art? It seems to me that much of the science fiction that deals with encounters with alien life forms asks about the ability to communicate, about the basic principles that are truly universal, symbolic abstract systems free of denotations, like mathematics, and doesn't really ask about what cannot be bridged, or transferred, since it's imminent to human experience. I think about Roger Zelazny's story, "A Rose For Ecclesiastes". It takes a different path and explores the ability to communicate with an alien culture based on its scriptures and lore. But in order to do so it assumes that the alien culture is anthropomorphic. On the other side, the literature that deals with unique qualities of human experience does so in relation to the computers, robots, androids, artificial beings, and there, the examination is based on a division between the intellectual and the emotional, the alleged rational and the irrational parts of the human psyche. A division I don't really accept in writing, and one I think that you also reject. I think that for you, ideas and intellectual constructs can be as emotional as any relationship drama or familial saga.

So, I'm a little weirded out by your claim that poetry is about honesty. For me writing has never been anything but honest. I see honesty as the courage to relentlessly and uncompromisingly explore yourself, the world as you come to know it, your biases, your prejudices. And you do it with any of the means at your disposal. Of course, you grow, you change, while writing. Existence, or fate or divinities, perfect or imperfect – take your pick – bombard you with mishaps, happiness, catastrophes, and you become sharper, keener, more able. Then you may judge a previous moment of honesty as a fake one, or not honest enough. But you keep on. And you develop; you search for new ways of expression. I'm using the general second person, but I mean you, Lavie, because I have seen you grow as writer, and what took courage in earlier works and was the goal of the work is now its self-evident starting point.

As for me, development meant letting go of the distinction between poetry and prose. I published two volumes of poetry, which were, I think, received well (several poems from these collections are part of the literature program for high schools in Israel, unfortunately). But I felt that much of my experience and interests don't find their way into my poetry, they are deemed unfit to serve as materials for poems. So I started writing essays, and my voice, as a writer, gained clarity on the one hand, but was, on the other, sterilised. I couldn't convey the emotional drama that accompanied my involvement in certain subjects – the metaphysical and philosophical grounds for speculative fiction, detective fiction, and their connections with poetry. So I moved to writing fiction. You'd assume that I'd turn to short stories. But I quickly found out that I express myself better in long form, novels mainly, and that the complexities of poetry, the endeavour of condensing layers of the language to the point that the ineffable is present, are to be had in novels. A novel for me is a poem unwrapped. Not just the verbal artefact that is the poem, but all the scaffolding and labour needed to bring it forth, from the abyss of the unconscious to the surface of expression.

I wonder if it is another reason for me to be obsessed with childhood and adolescence, if they are not the analogues of states of the shaping of the work, the very states in life of moving from potentiality to actuality, if they are not just the content, but the form of my work.

There are also political reasons for the obsession, as you so gently imply. There are always political reasons. But I believe that in mine these are subdued, and that your work addresses more directly the relationship between politics and literature. Your writing about Osama bin Laden and world terror is a clear example. There are lots of other examples, like your statement that Steampunk is "Fascism for nice people" that aroused a lot of indignation, and your short story "The School", that pointed out the colonial infrastructure of many of the human-alien encounters depicted in Western science fiction works. Do you think your heightened political sensibility is a result of your upbringing in a kibbuz, and of being able to identify the indoctrinating mechanisms in the Isareli *chinuch*? Is it part of the antagonism to the readymade nostalgia that's infused into Israeli culture? When you write political literature, what do you do – do you mourn the loss of possibilities, the loss of a more naïve self, or are you severing by it all contacts to the self that your teachers and parents worked so hard in manufacturing?

Lavie

I do strive for honesty, but I'm also painfully aware that I'm not being as honest as I can be in writing. We all have the parts of ourselves we want to keep hidden. Part of a writer's job is to explore those places, or transfigure them into fiction, but it's hard. I admire James Ellroy for doing it so completely, for so brutally putting himself on the page, but it's not something I feel I can do, not now, not to that extent.

I went from living on a kibbutz to living in South Africa at the transition year from Apartheid to democracy. In hindsight, this seems significant, though it may not have looked that at the time. The truth is, though, that I was never convinced by the stories I was told. I remember when I was eight years old or so, the kibbutz had one of their social evenings, with the host of an at-the-time well-known television programme – a sort of talk show, I suppose. And they asked for three generations of a kibbutz family to go on stage – my grandfather, my father and me. And when it came to me, Dalik – the presenter – asked whether, when I grow up, I intend to stay on the kibbutz.

And to everyone's horror, live on stage in front of the entire kibbutz, I said no. As far as I recall I said something like, "No, because there isn't enough privacy". I was eight!

And afterwards, all the founding members, the *vatikim*, as we call them, the kibbutz Elders, you know, they went up to my grandfather and kind of said, you know, what is it with your ideologically-suspect grandson?

I suppose I'll never honestly know why I was so drawn to weird fiction from a young age, and to science fiction and fantasy, but I think it might be because they were, at their best, so different to anything else. They were out there, they played with ideas, they tried everything. I think there was a period when science fiction was incredibly countercultural, but packaged in this gloriously strange and joyous bundle of story!

Whereas, on a kibbutz, there was only one right way to think. Which in itself is a sort of microcosmic reflection of wider Israeli society, I think. It's become actively dangerous to challenge the underlying beliefs of the state – our right to Israel, which is part God-given, part U.N-given, part "but they ran anyway" or "they never really lived here in the first place" or, my favourite, from a friend, "but they only lived here for 30 years earlier than us". I think what's interesting about this – it's sort of what this new novel is about, if I ever manage to write it – is that Herzl himself, the man who *founded* Zionism, was more interested in *a* homeland than *the* Holy Land. And the early Zionists wrote their own story of how *empty* the Holy Land was, that it had "but a small population of Arabs and fellahin and wandering, lawless, blackmailing Bedouin tribes". Which is as lovely a bit of propaganda writing as you could wish for. And yet the man who said this – Israel

Zangwill – himself became bitterly opposed to settlement in Palestine, realising that there was a large, settled Arab body there, and that conflict was going to erupt by the increase in Jewish settlement.

Yet here we are. I went on TV here a while back, to talk about the rocket attacks on Gaza last year, and the news anchor, a little sneeringly, said something like, "but you write science fiction, isn't that just escapism?"

To which I said, "but that is the best thing we can do, is try to imagine alternate realities, how else will we understand, or resolve, our own?"

I don't have *answers*, but it worries me when it becomes so that there are questions you can't even ask. That you're afraid – like I was in that interview – to say what you really think because the threat of violence is very real.

None of which, incidentally, makes for very good fiction, I should say! One of the reasons I find genre so liberating is that it's essentially, first, written for entertainment and, second, can get away with doing some pretty contentious things in the guise of being that harmless entertainment. I do seek to entertain, I do seek to anchor myself in story – if that means, à la Chandler, that a man must walk through the door with a gun, or, à la an editor I used to know, that you must always "start with a big explosion", well, this isn't just pulp fiction, this is also the world we live in. I like humour a lot. I think a lot of what I write is funny, because the humour works far better at showing off the real horror. Horror for its own sake is bland. For *A Man Lies Dreaming* I read a lot of jokes from the Holocaust, some of them very grim indeed – but humour is a powerful tool. I remember as kids, we'd tell Holocaust jokes in a hushed tone. It sounds awful, on the one hand, but on the other, it was a coping mechanism for us, to deal with this huge, awful *thing* that was placed on us. I don't know what it was like for you, but for me, it sometimes feels like my whole life was shaped by it, not when it was spoken about but in the absences, in the holes where it wasn't mentioned. I remember – I'm going for that emotional honesty thing again! – interrupting relatives on a visit one time, they were watching the news – the favoured Israeli pastime! – and I complained I was hungry.

And this uncle I had, he lost it. "Hungry? Hungry? Eat bread!" And I was ashamed. He survived Auschwitz, and here I was complaining?

It took me years to realise you could survive the camps but still be an asshole.

(This sounds awfully glib, I realise. But it's part of the dual way I was brought up I think. The silence around the survivors. The Israeli way of silently blaming them for surviving, while at the same time knowing, on some fundamental level, that these people experienced horrors the rest of us couldn't imagine – and so it's a mixture of guilt and suspicion, a toxic mix. Imagine being a child and having your life shaped with that).

I think every writer is political. It's just that some pretend not to be. Someone could say, I'm only writing about dragons and princes. But your politics is in everything. All the women raped in *Game of Thrones*, but no man ever suffers sexual violence – that's political. All the Israeli writers writing about affairs or divorces, aren't they just normalising Israel? If you do not write about Palestine, do you not simply erase it? Everything is a choice. I suppose, for me, anger is a motivation. I'd like to make a difference. Not for everyone. Maybe just for one person in particular. That kid who was me, sitting in a hidden corner of the library, between the Crime and Science Fiction shelves, nose buried in stacks of old magazines. That wonderful smell. That kid who knows something is wrong with reality, but he doesn't know what it is. That's all. Everything else – awards, reviews, money (ha!) – they're a distant second best.

Who do you write for, Shimon?

Shimon

I think you are right in presenting the question about the intended audience in relation to the political aspect of writing. My upbringing was, in details and social context, opposite to your own, yet as for the inner experience of growing up it had a similar pattern.

I grew up in Sderot, a small town, in a community that belonged the so-called Second Israel – a population that consisted of Jews who immigrated (or were brought, depending on the person you're asking) from Arab or Muslim countries. My parents were born in Morocco, and arrived in Israel at a young age, as part of the North African immigration waves of the 1950s. Their families were put in transition camps in the south of Israel, until development towns were erected, and the immigrants were given houses. But the government plans as to the future of the new population ended there, with no real thought about education or how the internal economics would work. As soon as my mother, for instance, graduated from the elementary school that was opened in Sderot, she was forced to look for a job. Because there were no high schools in the area, I mean, no high schools that received Mizrahi Jews (i.e. Jews from Arab countries, 'Mizrahi' meaning oriental) as students, and her family couldn't support her.

Like you, I spent my childhood and adolescence in a homogenous community, but what united the people in my community were not ideals, but the lack thereof – the deep sense of being deprived of the very basics that enable human beings to maintain a decent existence: their heritage was considered inferior and therefore deemed unworthy, their language barbaric and too close to the language of the Arab enemy. We were second-class citizens who had to be shaped properly before being allowed to participate in civil life. For in the meantime, the Mizrahi Jews were viewed as a tribal population, exotic to a certain extent. On one hand they kept the strong familial structure, and led a religious, almost messianic, life. On the other hand they were morally suspect, criminal in nature, uncommitted to the predominant ideology, Zionism, which was the true and only imminent solution for the modern, secular stage of Jewish existence.

The first generation of immigrant children, my parents' generation, grew up to be bitter, especially the men, who came from a male dominated society, whose main pride was in their big families and their ability to feed and educate their children. They were broken by the new conditions of living in Israel. They found jobs in the surrounding kibbutzim, and they suffered from serving as a manual labour force, without any prospects. They returned home angry, unfulfilled. And they unleashed, at least that's what my father did, their frustration, the rage born of being unimportant, on their children. Yet, it wasn't a simple construct. My father, for instance, adopted a double system of identification. On the outside, as he sought to get some recognition from his superior at the kibbutz factory he worked in, he became a Zionist, but a mutated form of Zionist, the right wing Zionism that Menachem Begin offered, perceiving the Jewish people not as idealists who were shaping their own fate, but as a group of victims, haunted, eternally despised, facing extinction. The life of the Israeli Jews was a constant struggle for survival. I can see the reasons for my father identifying with this world-view. But he didn't internalise it – on the inside, at home, he planned for his children to become rabbis. Not all of them. Only those who were inclined to reading and lacked real physical skills: his firstborn and then me.

My older brother rebelled quite early. He had some heated quarrels with my father, and one day took off his kippa, and said that he was no longer religious.

I took a different path of resistance. My father used to study with me, in the afternoon and evening, the Jewish scriptures, Mikra, Mishna, Talmud, the books of laws, I was made to learn long passages from them by heart, to quote, to relentlessly answer questions, who said what and why, what's the Halacha in this case, and what in another, why the difference in the approach of the various Jewish sages to the same case. Now, I love it. I draw great pleasure from breaking down the thought processes taking part in a Jewish debate of the law. As a child it was tedious, and full of fear. I was frightened. It seemed to me that I could only be loved under certain conditions, only when I could answer correctly the questions I was asked, only when I had the right answers. So I escaped, in the only way I know how, through other texts. I immersed myself in children's books that told about fantastical escapes from mundane life – children going on adventures, child detectives nosing around, children entering wonderlands through unexpected doors. And later on, science fiction, oh, stories and novels that told about travel in the expanses of space, meeting aliens, transfigurations, metamorphoses of the consciousness, becoming alien yourself, to everything you knew, being reborn. This literary experiment in identity and familiarity, it was crucial to me, since I was losing my faith, but the thirst for speculative thinking, for which I was conditioned, was never quenched. It was an opportunity to engage in philosophical thought through narratives and fiction (I loved stories back then, I still love them, even though I hate them so much, do you know what I mean?).

Reading became an inner sanctum. A sanctum from the discrimination against the Mizrahim. For the life of me I couldn't read literature dealing with the Ashkenazi malaises of retelling their self-made myths, their anguish, their experience of loss, their ongoing war to constitute a meaningful secular life. And it was a sanctum from my father's world, with his intentions to turn me into some person I couldn't be, to carry with me the flames of his ire, the burden of his Jewish sages agonising in their places of learning over the status of an egg that was laid during a Holy Day.

When I wrote my first poems, I just wanted to stay in this sanctum: if I imagined readers, I imagined them in similar sancta. I wrote about life in Sderot and I wrote about my family as I would write nature poems, about the beauty of the forsaken and desolate, about the elation one can achieve once facing the essence of forsakenness. But when I published them, I was struck by the responses. They were read as principally political, as representative of the state of the Mizrahim. I wasn't the only Moroccan second-generation writer. But as my peers were intentionally protesting, producing social realist work, my interest was, and still is, in speculative writing, in, as you put it, imagining alternate worlds. And as the pressure to put forth works that deal directly with the damages done to Jews from Arab countries grew, I retreated deeper and deeper into my sanctum – I write for readers who defy ready-made categories of identity and experience and their ready-made modes of representation. Yet, I'm vigilant in giving form to my past, to my parents' silenced heritage, even to the unkind memories of studying with my father, of the gnashing of teeth.

There are two forms of being political in writing, you see. One is to adhere to what's considered political, to take part in what is defined as the political discourse. In that manner, being political is dealing with representations, the right ones, the wrong ones, the crooked and the correct. The other manner is to reject the decree of the Polis, of the community, and to do away with the mere notion of representing.

What I like about your work is the way it oscillates between the two forms, and how wild it becomes in its shift between the two when it deals with modern Jewish and Ashkenazi-Israeli foundations of identity. I think it is most apparent when you write about the main source of its current phase, the Holocaust. Why do you think it became so central? How can literature diffuse it without defiling it?

Lavie

I remember when I came back to Israel in 2010, when we met – I didn't realise, I think, just how divided Israeli society is based on where you come from. On one's ethnicity, really, despite this idea that Israel is the great melting pot. And that's interesting in itself – the term comes from a play by Israel Zangwill, who I mentioned earlier. And Zangwill applied it to America, which he called, "God's Crucible, the great Melting-Pot where all the races of Europe are melting and reforming."

Everyone is supposed to be one thing, Jewish, but in fact it's a far more divided country than some, I think. And that was a genuine culture shock for me. And as someone who hadn't lived in Israel for, I think, twenty years by that time, it felt very uncomfortable to be addressed as a representative of a certain group, of a plural *You* – it felt very antagonistic. Which is I think something that is difficult to explain to an outsider. We're *supposed* to be this great Jewish nation, but it more often feels like a group of people with not necessarily much in common, thrown together to get along as best they could. And I know you very much resisted being typecast as a spokesperson for Moroccan Jews, for an *us* – which I think is a real danger in Israeli society. That pressure to conform, to be a part of a group. I found the concept of the *gibbush*, when I was growing up – which is this thing where they take a group of young kids and throw them together and attempt to create a unit out of them, in preparation for the army – I found that very disconcerting when I was young, and I find it that way now – when I'm a little less young! And it's a danger for writers, because you have to speak for yourself, not for others. And it's easy to be seduced. To accept an award, to become a spokesperson, and eventually you become a part of the group, a part of this story that we want to present to the world. I remember you saying once about the Israeli writers who became successful overseas, in translation – our great Spokesmen, for they are always men of a certain kind – how their writing became writing for translation. There is that insidious form of government sponsored propaganda in Israel, the *Hasbara*, the great project of *explaining*, a campaign to justify and promote Israel and what it does to the foreign media, and it's almost a responsibility to do so – and yet you wonder why it's needed. If we really have nothing to justify...

Outside Israel, I suppose, you're just a Jew. In Israel, I'm Ashkenazi, I'm a kibbutznik, I'm – an assortment of labels, depending on the situation. So in a way, I feel a bit like James Joyce. I need to be an exile in order to write about home.

I needed to live there again for a while, and several of my projects really began there – particularly my Central Station cycle of stories, inspired by Tel Aviv's old bus station area, which is inhabited now by African refugees and Asian economic migrants, and a lot of what's going into this new novel, which is explicitly about the competing narratives of Israel and Zionism.

Which takes me back to the question of audience. I think you have really explored yourself – who you are, what *forms* you – in a novel like *Mox Nox* in particular, which delves into growing up in Sderot, the contrast with the kibbutzim around it, the relationship with your father. And in a way I envy you, because we have essentially different tasks. You write for an audience that implicitly knows some of what you write. For better or worse, you write in Hebrew, for an Israeli audience. Whereas I can't even get published in Israel! If I want to write about the kibbutz, say, I have to explain it, I have to do the – to use that awful term – 'world building', as if I were describing an alien planet.

When Nir Yaniv and I were writing *The Tel Aviv Dossier*, in English, we added little explanations here and there in sentences, a comma and a line after a term, that sort of thing. And when it was translated into Hebrew, we could go over it and take all those little flags down! And for me, a lot of writing is a question of how much do you explain. And I hate explaining. But it's a balancing act.

I find it easier to write about Israel in short fiction, because I feel more freedom in that form. I find it easier to publish, you can take more chances – with style, with subject matter. This new novel I keep talking about actually borrows from a lot of stories I wrote over the past few years – from "Uganda", "The Time-Slip Detective", "Shira" – all short stories about alternate Zions, both utopian and dystopian. And I'm getting very excited about it now. But at the same time, I think, who in their right mind is going to *buy* this book? Will it even be published? I picture the acquisition meeting at a publishers, the faces of a lot of nice British people looking bemused, thinking, He's writing *what*? Who *cares*?

Which is a very roundabout way of getting to your question about the Holocaust, I suppose. Because I did write that book, finally – *A Man Lies Dreaming* – and that was one of the hardest things I've ever had to do. Not just the writing of it, but the question of whether it will get published – I have to give my editor, and my agent, full props for pushing it and believing in it. But I wasn't sure it was going to be published until about 3 months before the actual publication date. It was close. And I do feel I struggle more now. Because what I want to write is difficult. I want it to still be story-structured – I want it to be exciting, and funny, and all of those things – but I need it to matter. I need it to be painful, difficult, to push people's buttons. Which goes back to representation, in a way, to being a spokesperson. I don't want to do that! I see literature as an act of unbalancing, as a challenge. It needs to upset people, it needs to *push*. It needs, I think, to be uncomfortable. It shouldn't *please*.

Yet at the same time, of course, I come from, and I love, genre fiction. I want to be entertained. I like the lurid, the low art, the dingy dives, the shadows. I like sleaze.

Writing *A Man Lies Dreaming* (which has all of those things!), was not a question of how do I write it. It was a question of, how can I *not* write it? I mean, no one wanted it. It was unsellable. "What's it about?" my agent said. And I said, "Adolf Hitler: Private Eye". And I remember his reaction. That brief, shocked look and then that genuine laughter.

He thought it was great! And he told me there was no way he could sell it.

It sounds like a bad joke, which of course is part of the whole thing. But I figured if anyone could get away with it, it might be me. But I tried to not write it. I tried to write other books, and I couldn't. I was running out of options. And then one night I just gave in. I said, no one needs to know. I'll just sit here, and I'll just write the first line, and see what happens. And if it fails, no one needs to know! And I wrote, "She had the face of an intelligent Jewess". Which is a slightly modified line from Chandler, from *The Big Sleep*, and I was dying to write it for so long. The casual racism in that one line. And I couldn't stop. I wrote the book, and then I rewrote it, and rewrote it, and amazingly it got published. But the actual *writing* part of it? That first draft? That was the easiest thing I ever wrote. Only *Osama* came close to it. But it messed me up. I wrote it late at night, very quickly. You write quickly too, I know. I'm usually much slower, but I needed to get it out of myself as quickly as possible. I loved writing Wolf, my loser Hitler. Hitler as the Big Lebowski. Writing someone who was so *angry* all the time. Someone who hated, so much, so deeply – and yet was entirely powerless to do anything about it, which is of course where a lot of the humour comes from.

We write, I think, to air our demons. And for me, the Holocaust is that big black hole in the centre of my life. It shapes everything. I have a very fatalistic attitude. I can't grow an attachment to things, to ownership. I can't settle, I have to keep moving. I know how quickly it can all be taken.

My mother was born in a refugee camp near Munich, after the war. Her parents survived Auschwitz. I think they met in the refugee camp, though I'm not sure. Auschwitz broke something inside them which didn't make for good parents.

She didn't have a happy childhood. They emigrated to Israel when she was two. My grandfather, on my father's side, left Transylvania when he was eighteen. He was a Zionist. He left everything to come to Palestine, to found the kibbutz. They lived in tents, they worked for the Jewish farmers. He met my grandmother and they moved into a tent together. I was very close to him. But he lost all his family in the Holocaust. Two sisters survived. One in Auschwitz, at fourteen. The other hiding for three years in an apartment in Budapest, looked after by a non-Jewish friend who saved her life. What kind of a life is that?

So I'm third generation. I'm shaped by silences. By absences. I went to Transylvania. Did I ever tell you that? When I was seventeen, I went backpacking in Europe. I stayed with Gabor, the man who saved my grandfather's sister all those years before, and then I went to the town my grandfather grew up in. I'm the only one in the family to ever do it. I went back to the cemetery where my great great grandfather lives. His name was Adolf Heizikovics.

How is that for irony? Hitler even managed to ruin the name.

Everyone there was transported to the camps. They're not buried in the cemetery. There was nothing to bury. There's a memorial wall, with their names. And I remember as a child, doing a Roots project, you know, where you find out about where your family came from, having to go to see my grandmother and ask her about the camps. A boy of ten, maybe. Eleven. I remember how uncomfortable I was. And she tried to tell me. But how do you tell the Holocaust?

I was struck by how uniform the testimonies I read were. I craved giving them a voice. To force them on other people, to make people face up to it. You know, the Holocaust – stuff like the Holocaust happens all the time. It wasn't unique to the Germans. What's so chilling about the Nazis, though, was how precise it all was. How *industrial*. You'd think mass murder, ethnic cleansing – you think it's done in anger, in hate. But the Nazis *automated* it. They didn't *feel* one way or the other about it. They just got on with it. It was a *job*. I think that's the real horror. It wasn't the killing fields – it was a bloody bureaucracy. That's what's chilling about it.

But Israel, we hold it up like a justification, now. It's our trump card. We can justify *anything* with the Holocaust. It disgusts me. Did we learn nothing? Did we not learn, at the very least, some *compassion*? What is Gaza if not a ghetto? My family lost their homes, they lost everything, they were not allowed back, those who survived. Yet we deny the Palestinians the same right of return. How can you justify injustice with injustice? Death with death?

A Man Lies Dreaming is about the Holocaust, but it's really about the rise of the *kind* of hatred the Nazis had. The one that says *you are different, and therefore you are less*. The anti-immigrant rhetoric of right wing Europe. The anti-Islamic messages in Europe now. And it's a funny book, too, because what else are you going to do? You can laugh, or you can cry. I remember, years ago, an Israeli bus driver. Somewhere in the Negev, by the side of the road. It was very hot. And he said, "I would rather a thousand Palestinian children died than to see one dead Jewish child."

And sure, it's a bit of a rhetoric, it almost sounds funny, doesn't it? But what were the rocket attacks on Gaza last year but exactly that? It made his words sound like a prophecy. I should have known to listen to the voices one hears in the desert.

But I'm not sure I answered your question. Ask me again

later, maybe. I sound, even to myself, very angry, when usually I am such a nice person... I don't like confrontation. I'm not very Israeli that way. I go out of my way to avoid conflict. One thing I always figured out was, I'm not a hero. I would have gone to the camps. What else could I have done? Heroes belong in movies, not in real life. And this is another thing that bothers me, how we celebrate 'heroes' now. By which we mean violence. When did our heroes become soldiers? When did we begin to glorify death, like we do with the fanatics of Masada?

The notion of the hero is very interesting to me. I did write a book about it, after all. The super-hero. I don't think I ever asked you this, whether it came up in any of our conversations. How do you see the hero, specifically, in your work? Is that something you think about?

Shimon

I don't really know why you are afraid of rage. You are not righteous or scary, but sharper and clearer. I advocate pure cleansing rage as a motivation for writing. We tried to have this conversation before, during the War on Gaza last summer, and we were both depressed, unable to find the energies to talk. We lost our faith in communication or in the ability of literature to mind, to facilitate any change in the consciousness of the readers, even though we both were mutated by literature, matured while weaving pieces of the books we read into our life experiences. Yet, the rage I felt during the war was a vital one, awakening. I wrote in amok, rabidly. The rage enabled me to write something I thought impossible – a sequel.

It sounds funny, but it isn't. I consider my first novel, *One Mile and Two Days before Sunset*, to be a somewhat naïve, raw work. But Elish Ben Zaken, the main character, the unwilling detective, never stopped bothering me. By dealing with him, and with the murder investigation that was forced on him, that lured him to figure out places in himself he thought he repressed successfully, I was trying to address an issue in Jewish-Israeli life – how can one know what is beautiful, what is truthful, and still be morally paralysed? What is this state of moral paralysis that permeates Israeli society?

Elish was able to avoid facing moral issues. He was quite cunning about it – he defines himself as a "clerk of small human sins", i.e. he took cover in plain sight. It wasn't that he waved away morality, just that he reduced it to cases in which taking a moral standpoint does not undermine his convictions about justice, doing justice. Did you know that Israel has one of the largest animal rights activist communities? Did you know that the population of vegans here is growing rapidly? Did you hear about the vegetarian soldiers' struggle to have military kitchens altered to meet their dietary restrictions? The absurdity, the historical ironies involved, are sometimes too much.

I picked up this Elish, who, in a way, is a reflection of myself, of the man I maybe am, and if not, the man I fear to become, and I threw him into the middle of a murder investigation. What do you do with a clever guy who solves the mystery, finds the culprit, but refuses to act upon his knowledge? My novel ended there, with his refusal to take part in any justice system, be it human and therefore corrupt and made to serve those in power, or be it divine and cruel and unforgiving.

This last war, and the crude forces that were in play to silence any criticism against it, by violence and fake declarations of emergency status to achieve civil obedience, filled me with rage, fuelled me. I couldn't anymore turn away from

Elish, and what he represents in my life. I couldn't anymore avoid asking him, what would you do now? Is the picture less murky for you now to commit, to choose sides, to be ready to exert justice? I didn't even have to delve into the tedious craft of working out a story, of constructing a narrative. Once I had the question, the motivation, the fuel, I had the tone, the music, and I just sped through it. I didn't meet any obstacle along the way. Nonetheless, the central mystery, that was supposed to be the principal device to make Elish confront his values and choices, eluded me. The mystery was as to the nature of the mystery: of all the riddles Elish came across, which is the one that needed solving? So Elish took off, once again, to pondering about the religious and existential implications of the desire to investigate.

You see, he is summoned to solve the mystery of a girl who disappeared on her way to Sderot, was absent for three days and then returned with no memory as to her whereabouts. This time around, his family is living in Sderot, he has to make his way through bombarded streets, has to investigate people who are willing to have him sanctioned for being a leftie traitor, and yet he leaves off contemplating the structure of the world and the will to know, to understand. Is there a point to self-beating?

I wish I knew. Instead I can console myself with trying to understand the reason for this unforeseeable twist. It has to do with your question about heroes and heroism.

Evidently I don't care much about the heroic model that Israeli culture and society have to offer. They are militant in nature. The main initiation rite in Israel is the army service. Now, there you have your real melting pot, for good and for bad. For many young Jewish men and women, the mandatory army service is the first period in life when they leave their parents' home, meet with other young people from social and economic strata they have only heard of, and sometimes from ethnic groups they only see on TV. It's where the great divisions that are quite kept even within Jewish majority are breached. At the age they are most open to influence, they sometimes undergo some of the most extreme experiences of their life.

So the first model of heroism I encountered in school and in the YA literature of the time is the brave, patriotic soldier (or, more monstrously than that, children who wish to grow up to serve their country, and meanwhile act as spies of their own volition and fight the Arabic threat in their spare afternoons). This model, as you pointed out, was created by the Zionist ideology and was stretched backward in time, to the eras of Jews living under Greek and Roman occupation, and to biblical times: the heroes that lived by their sword, the fanatics who preferred to obliterate all that was around them and, if things weren't going their way, according to their faith, chose to burn and be burnt.

The second model I had to deal with came from religious life, from the teaching of the great Jewish Sages, of the Mishna and the Talmud, often referred to as Chazal. For them, heroism was mostly intellectual and spiritual – Shimon Ben Zoma (who, by the way, is the unsung Jewish hero in the background of my *Rose of Judea* trilogy) famously stated: "Who is a hero – the one who vanquishes his appetites". My childhood was filled with stories about Talmidey Ha'chamim, who achieved supernatural powers by studying the Jewish scriptures, who could turn rivers to ash, raise storms, make miracles, but they abstained from any action, knowing that interfering with the world won't end well, that acceptance is the only suitable reaction.

In the Babylonian Talmud there is a much-discussed story that illustrates this point, *The Oven of Akhnai*. It's unclear what this oven is, whether it belonged to a man called Akhnai, or whether it was shaped in the form of an Akhan, which is a species of snake. The sages debated if it was pure. Rabbi Eliezer Ben Horkenus, who was one of the strictest, most ultra-orthodox sages of the Mishna, claimed it was and brought forth every argument possible. The other sages said it wasn't. In fear of losing the debate, Rabbi Eliezer began performing miracles to prove his position, ordering a carob tree to grow in Beit Ha-midrash, a stream of water to go backward, the walls of Beit Ha-midrash to fall down. And the sages said, again and again, no proof can be made this way. Then he called heaven for help. A voice came out of heaven and declared that Rabbi Eliezer, in fact, was always right. To which Rabbi Yehoshua answered – it is not in heaven. It is not up to heaven to decide. This story is usually read as a parable about asserting the authority of the Sages over human affairs by forbidding divine intervention.

I read it differently. What Rabbi Eliezer did was open the possibility of Judaism interfering with the world. If you have the powers to change reality for you own goals, why not use it? Why not improve the life of Jews under a foreign regime, vindicate them? Because it never ends there, there is always a price to pay. Rabbi Eliezer was excommunicated for not accepting the decision of the sages. If you go on and read the story, you find out that in his sorrow he kills, just by praying and imploring heaven, his brother-in-law, who served as the Head of Sages at the time.

I took, and still take, the term for intellectual excellence in the Talmud – "unrooting mountains and grinding them against each other" – quite literally. The great rabbis are capable of the deed. And yet it's not a model I can adopt either. The two opposing models are also expressions of two concurrent types of Judaism: the historical Judaism and the traditional Judaism. The first one agrees to be part of history and obey its demands, the infrastructure of identity that history imposes on it. For Jews of this type, being a victim, surviving anti-Semitism in all its forms, the founding of the state of Israel, becoming "a modern nation as any other nation", are the defining facts and moments of Jewish existence.

Traditional Judaism has nothing to do with history. It happens all the time, but does affect Jews of this type. Being a Jew is participating in the Jewish conversation that started when reality came into being and will end when reality is redeemed. Everything else is a distraction, an obstacle.

I can only view myself as a person who is torn between these two models, these two worldviews. My characters are more decisive than me, though decisiveness is never their strongest suit. They are plunged into a setting – speculative or fantastical – in which they must act according to the first model, if they are to save the people important to them, or to fight for their values and freedom, but discover that the second model is the one applicable to them, even if it means losing everything. They could be superheroes, if only they were able to accept super-heroism as a form of action. But if they would, they wouldn't have interested me in the first place.

What about your characters? You mentioned before that Joe in *Osama* is adrift. Fogg in *The Violent Century*, as his name implies, is a superhero working in the shadows. He is more a British secret agent than a superhero. On the other hand, you wrote the chronicles of Gorel, a sword and sorcery kind of action hero (and much fun to read about). I'm intrigued as to the pull of the two polls of heroism, and intrigued as to their literary parallels – can writing be thought of as a sort of heroism? And if so, do you have an ethos of heroism you aspire writing to follow?

Lavie

I think what you bring up about detective fiction is quite interesting. There's a story I'm fascinated by, partly perhaps because I can't actually *read* it. It's by a Russian writer – one of the Jewish SF writers who emigrated to Israel, I think – and it's a traditional murder mystery. It's set in a theatre, and there's a murderer, and there's a detective, and near the end of the book, the detective solves the crime.

Only, the book is set in the Warsaw Ghetto. And as soon as the detective finds the killer, everyone gets shipped to Auschwitz – murderer, detective and all – and there they die.

One of the essays I am most obsessed with – that I keep riffing off of, and parodying too – is Raymond Chandler's famous "The Simple Art of Murder", which sets out the classic image of the detective, the hero. Chandler's hero is a classic white knight; he does "the right thing" at whatever the cost. But what is the right thing? What *is* a hero?

I am not much interested in heroes, but perhaps I am interested in the iconography of heroism. It's there in *The Violent Century*, which tries to interrogate that very primal icon of the 'superhero', which was born out of the shadow of the Second World War, and weirdly enough in *A Man Lies Dreaming*, which turns Hitler, of all people, into the parody of Chandler's famous hero, Philip Marlowe. And I think I love the detective formula because it demands a certain sort of action. My characters, left to themselves, would be reflections of me: Hamlets stuck in inaction, forever agonising over what to do, where to go, until they end up going nowhere, doing nothing. A detective has to *act*. Moreover, he has to ask questions, which I think is something we don't often think much about necessarily. There is something incredibly *liberating* about the plot of a detective novel. It's a form of questioning. It is incredibly flexible, in that way. And the reason that I am not a crime fiction writer is that, to me, the *least* interesting thing is who the murderer is. I mean, who *cares*!

I read a lot of crime for entertainment. I don't really ask for much! I tend to read series. I suppose most people do. But when I look at a typical crime shelf, I have no idea why most of them bothered. The books look cloned. They are formula for formula's sake. They are well written, but they do not exceed the parameters of the formula. Whereas Chandler, say, pushed the formula, he twisted it to suit himself. He was not interested in the solution: he was interested in the journey. (He said once that a good detective book would still work if you lost the last eight pages. That is, the solution should never matter.) Which is why, although I use the crime fiction formula for my purposes, I would also make a terrible crime writer. I don't care about the resolution. In *A Man Lies Dreaming*, even you pushed me to tighten the mystery plot element of the book! Wolf, my detective, is supposedly looking for a missing Jewish woman in London in 1939, and also trying – rather half-heartedly – to uncover a Jewish plot to assassinate Oswald Mosley, the leader of the British Fascists. But these were, for me, purely the device, the engine to motivate Wolf, to make him go on his journey. The mystery is banal. I resolved it at the end, almost incidentally. But both you and my editor wanted more, so I tightened it a little bit, so it was a little more central: but the fact was that Wolf just wasn't a very good detective.

A good example of this is in the book I've been working on, where the engine is, again, the search for a missing girl. And

I had to write a synopsis for the book – which is pretty much impossible for me, since I'm one of those writers who prefer to discover the book while I'm writing it. But I gave it a shot. And then I sat on it, and when I went back, I read through it, and I realised, you get to the end, and I completely failed to mention what happened to the missing girl! It just wasn't very important. That's formula, it's pulp (anyway, I went back and added it in, but again, it's a sort of incidental 'resolution'). I always think of the chauffeur in *The Big Sleep*. Someone murders him but if you look closely you realise, in the end, we have no idea who did it. Chandler just forgot about it. It's just... it's just how life is. No one cared who killed the chauffeur.

I think when crime writing is done well, it can be an incredibly powerful tool. It's interesting that Israel never had much of a crime writing tradition. I suppose it would have been too much against the sort of ruling narrative. And when it did come in, I think a book like Batya Gur's *Murder On a Kibbutz* was incredibly powerful. It was an examination, a critique, of this unique social structure. And I was very fond of the early Shulamit Lapid novels, set in Be'er Sheva, which make good use of their environment.

But I was still unsatisfied. They still did not offer a genuine challenge. They did not *question* the main narrative of Israel, which is what I am driven to do, and which is what this novel I've been trying to write is explicitly about. We're talking about heroes, and like I said, I grew up with the heroes of Israel – do you know the story of Trumpeldor? I'm a kid, and this is the stuff I'm being offered, what I need to look up to. This is the kind of story that shapes me. Trumpeldor was a decorated Russian soldier. He lost his arm to shrapnel (in the Russo-Japanese War, I just Googled that). And he was a proud Zionist. He made Aliyah, and he became a Shomer (and there's a reason my pulp writer in *A Man Lies Dreaming* is named Shomer!), which means Guardian, Guard. And famously, he took charge of the defences of Tel Hai, a Jewish settlement in the Galilee, which came under attack from Arab marauders. And Trumpeldor, the one-armed defender, protected the settlement, despite being grievously wounded in battle. And as he lay dying, in the arms of his comrades, he opened his eyes and said, "Never mind, it is good to die for our country". And then he died.

What did Wilfred Owen call it? "The old lie"? *Dulce et decorum est, pro patria mori.*

Trumpeldor *is* the Zionist hero. The hero of my childhood. The hero whose later reincarnation is Yoni Netanyahu dying in Entebbe. All of our heroes are dead.

And I think it bothered me even as a child. *Why* is it good to die for our country? Wouldn't it be better to *live* for it? What is a country *for*? Shouldn't the country be for the people, and not the people for the country?

And was that really such a radical idea? All my life I knew I was destined to grow up; to serve in the army; to carry a gun. But – and rather selfishly! – I didn't want to!

The editor Didi Chanoch once called this body of stories and myth the "Matter of Israel", after the same term for the British legends of King Arthur and so on, and that really stuck with me. We have not really explored that body, and not critically. It's something I want to do more of – I'm fascinated with the story of N.I.L.I., for instance, the Jewish spy ring that operated during the time of Ottoman rule. It embodies a lot of how our notions of heroism were later formulated. It's a period I'm drawn to, a period when the Matter of Israel was still being formed.

One of my favourite works is a short novella I did, *Jesus*

& *The Eightfold Path*. (Which, strangely enough, was acciden-tally translated not once but twice into Hebrew, and then never published in Israel at all!) Anyway, it's about the life of Jesus. It was based on this idea I had that the three Wise Men from the East were the same companions of the Buddha in the Chinese classic *A Journey To The West*. It made sense! So they travel to Judea to find the Buddha – the infant Jesus – and they spirit him away to Egypt, and train him in kung fu...

No, I know, it *is* very silly!

Anyway, it sticks pretty close to Matthew. There's some weird stuff in the source material – demons, the devil, all kinds of stuff! And it made sense that when he was in Egypt (which Matthew gets rid of in a single sentence), Jesus met the young Cleopatra...

Anyway. The point of all this is that, in the middle of the book, the point of view changes, and we realise the narrator – who then becomes an observer/actor in the story – is Jose-phus Flavius, the Romano-Jewish historian. He was born Yosef Ben Matityahu, in Jerusalem, and commanded the out-post of Yodfat, in the Galilee, during the first Jewish-Roman War. And what happened in Yodfat was almost the exact same thing that happened in Masada. Roman forces laid siege to the town. Josephus and his men hid in a cave as the town was overrun, its citizens slaughtered. The men – like in Masada – decided to kill themselves rather than surrender, and drew lots to kill each other. Josephus was the last to remain, and he promptly surrendered to the Romans. He eventually became a Roman citizen, a celebrated historian and a close advisor of both Vespasian and his son, Titus. He died of old age.

And as I was writing this, the story of Jesus became the story of Josephus, which then became the question: What is a Jew?

And it seems to me that to us, to modern day Israelis, the image of Josephus would be a loathsome one. He was a traitor and a coward – and yet he *lived*.

And wasn't that the essence of being a Jew? How does it go, at every holiday meal? "They tried to kill us. They failed. Let's eat."

A lot of what we know about the Great Revolt, the Fall of Jerusalem, the fate of the Jews of that time, comes from Josephus. He lived. He remained. He witnessed. We don't remember the men who killed each other in Yodfat. We remember Josephus.

To me, Josephus represents the great schism between being an Israeli and being a Jew. Josephus is the first of the exiles, the usherer of the *Golah*, the Diaspora. Israel was a project of re-engineering a new kind of Jew. The Sabra. We rejected everything of the old ways, of the Diaspora. We shed our names, our language. We changed the names of old streets to reflect the new reality we wished to live in. Take Jamal Pasha Avenue in Jaffa, the main road that cuts through the city. You and I both lived on either side of it, after all. It was built during the Ottoman rule of Palestine. Then the British came, and it became King George. Then, when Jaffa was taken by the Jewish forces – in what we call The War of Independence, the Palestinians call the Nakba, or the Catastrophe, and the rest of the world carefully calls 'The 1948 War' – its name was changed to No. 1 Street. Finally, when Tel Aviv and Jaffa were united, the new administration renamed it to Jerusalem Avenue (Sderot Yerushalayim). Nir Yaniv once told me that when he first moved to Tel Aviv, he lived in a confluence of streets all named after pogroms! I worked this into the story, "Tutim", that's included here. I'm fascinated by psychogeography.

I'd love to know who was in charge of naming streets. They certainly weren't subtle! There's so much power in that. Naming is a sort of shaping. There's a novel there...

To me, this new reality – this enforced reality – is endlessly fascinating. I can't help but see reality as a construct, as a fiction. A story. And so I worry at it, I try to interrogate it in the only way I know how, which is by telling stories of my own. Maybe that's why all my stories are meta-stories – they know they are artifice, artefacts, that a story *cannot* be real.

But I'm curious, because the geography – the psychogeography – is also, I think, important to you – in *Kfor* you use the landscape and the street names of Jaffa quite consciously, in your story of an isolated Jewish enclave in a post-human future. And you also have – I don't know if I should be saying this! – the habit of setting at least a scene in whatever flat you happen to live in during the writing of the novel... so the flat where the mysterious 'unlicensed poet' first appears in *Kfor* was your flat in Jaffa, for instance (and that's also something referenced in my own "Tutim", included in this book, and which opens in the flat I used to live in, in Jaffa – see? I can't help the obscure reference!).

Was this something you were conscious of, the geography, the names, when you were writing? And also, digging up some reviews of *Kfor* in the Israeli media, I see you are accused, over and over again, of being "too demanding", of "showing off" with quotes and references (something that, alas, I have some experience with myself). I'm not going to ask you what you think about that, but rather – since it's a question that occupies me – what is the role of the reference? What is its purpose, and why do we use it?

Shimon

Let me start with a reference. We both, in some of our work, individually, adopt a technique, that I suspect is derived from Samuel Delany's *The Einstein Intersection* – embedding the circumstances of writing in the work itself. Writers always kept writing journals, in which they documented their doubts, made notes as to the construction of the work, its goal, the calculations behind the decision making, and sometimes the physical condition of writing. But they tended to keep them apart from the work. In *The Einstein Intersection* Delany integrates these scaffolds so nonchalantly into the narrative of the novel, so seamlessly. This is first a tribute to him, and to the many ways he influenced my writing – I write my answer on my way to Israel from the U.S., in Philadelphia airport, in the wake of a snowstorm hitting the East Cost, it is night time and the snow on the ground is grey, but glowing through the dark.

When I leave Israel I experience conflicting sensations – once I lay my feet on foreign soil, I know how little I'm going to miss Israel. Yet, after two days of hearing and speaking languages other than Hebrew, my sense of reality starts to dim. It begins with how fake other sounds sit in my aural organs, the mouth or the ear. The sounds are heavy, unnatural. After that the surrounding seems to be makeshift, a layer of well-produced and -executed mirage. Do you remember the story in *The Martian Chronicles*, about Martians projecting to the Earth crew members (really, to the Americans seeking to colonise Mars) their own innermost longings? Something in that vein. And the only method of stabilising reality is speaking Hebrew. Moreover, thinking myself in Hebrew.

I do believe that we don't have any ideas before they are articulated in a symbolic system, and I do believe that dif-

54

ferent languages offer different nuances of articulating the world and self-experience. I cling, woefully, to the set of nuances of Hebrew.

You alluded to the benefits of writing in Hebrew, but there are major downsides. If you are politically aware, then it's a constant struggle. Writing in Hebrew forces you to take a stand towards the history of Hebrew literature. Formulating modern Hebrew literature played a major part in the effort to create a secular, national identity for Jews in Europe. It was conceived as an intersection of three issues: the linguistic (Hebrew), the nationalistic (the identity of the modern Jewish nation at first and later on – Zionism and Israeli nationality), and the religious (its approach to Judaism – was it a natural continuation of writing liturgical poetry, philosophy and books of Halacha, or a negation of those?). No separation between the aspects was made. Asking a question in one aspect required answers in the other two as well. This kind of identity between the aspects permeates all writing in Hebrew. We say Hebrew literature, but what we mean is actually Jewish-Israeli-Hebrew literature. It's weird, even works that are written in Hebrew and don't have anything to do with the existence of Israel or with Judaism are included in the matrix; they become, by context, tacitly Jewish-Israeli-Hebrew.

Once you notice this simple fact, you can oppose it or you can celebrate it. But whatever action you take, I discovered, you validate this identity, you admit it is natural and historically true. For me, I can only work with it by writing along the fissure lines of the identity – tracing what they cover while smoothing and yet insinuating alleged truths when they are unavoidable.

Kfor was the first work where I was knowingly doing it. The idea of the book, or at least its tone, its underlying atmosphere, was born out of an outlandish experience. I was going through a hard period of mourning. During that period I went back to Sderot, and to praying in the synagogue of my childhood. The boys I grew up with were now men, they stayed in Sderot, married, had children. Most of them lived in the vicinity of their parents' houses. Their sons looked the same way they used to look as boys. So much changed, and still time had no effect. At first I felt like I was living in two separate times, past and present, overlapping. And afterwards I realised that this is how Jews have been living for centuries, that the repetition is ritualistic in nature, that it's the traditional form of denouncing the demands of history.

So I planned to write a book about a Jewish community, 500 years in the future, still reliving its past, addicted to it. The society depicted in it is ultra orthodox; as a matter of fact, it's a society trying to live according to the Mishnaic code of conduct. I return to era of the Mishna, which was one of the most formative eras in Judaism as we know it, one of the most productive and creative, when Judaism was a raw thought, embryonic, and the boundaries of Jewish identity were still fluid. It's not a big surprise that the sages of the Talmud, the children of the next era in Jewish orthodoxy, were fascinated with the possibility of important figures in the Mishnaic era having gentile roots, and the erotic tension between other important Tanaim (Sages of the Mishna) and Roman women of aristocrat stature. One clear example is the Midrash claiming that Shema'ia and Avtalion, the mythological two Sages at the dawn of the Mishnaic era, were the descendants of Sanherib, the Assyrian ruler. Another emblematic example is the Midrash telling how Rabbi Akiva, the figure after which the Mishnaic method was fashioned, came to wed Rufina, the wife of Quintus Tineius Rufus, the Roman governor of the province of Judea.

So, starting with the question of denouncing history and the question of formulating Jewish identity, taking down the Jewish-Israeli-Hebrew triad, was imminent. Nationalism is a product of historic understandings, and these were irrelevant.

But of course, I had to ask my questions not in an abstract manner, but through the experience and perspectives of individuals living in this future Jewish theocracy, and starting to picture them to myself I had to ask about their language, what would their Hebrew sound like, how would it behave, now that the confinements of Israeli Hebrew are put aside.

The novel is based on a trick. It is told by a narrator who lives in the current Israel, but he is a poet in great need of finding his own language, as for him the solid, firm Hebrew of Hebrew literature is hollow. I, as a writer, and he, Doron Aflalo, as the narrator, searched to recreate the moments of the birth of Hebrew, the modes in which it was shaped into a spoken language, when it was still a patchwork of biblical grammar and Mishnaic innovation of legal terms and medieval incorporation of philosophical concepts and the 19th century introduction of mundane vocabulary. And I tried to show how clumsily it is being brought together. There is no way I could have done it without a ton of references to Jewish scripture, some of them obscure. It wasn't easy for me to figure it out, so why would it be different for the readers? Understanding your language and culture is an excruciating experience and I'm repeating myself, but I don't care – literature for me is about the transmission of experience.

Speaking about experience, here I am, sitting on the plane. The pilot got stuck in traffic due to the snowstorm and while waiting for him to arrive, the wings froze and deicing is in progress. More dead time. More dead time - I think there is another reason for my insistent referencing. I wish to write literature that is primarily Jewish-Hebrew, though I know I have to work hard to show where it differs from Israeli literature and where it adheres to its basic pattern. And if I have to stay true to my mission, I need to accept the fact that it is a precarious literature, that it can only exist as a part of a conversation, in which everything is not a real time or a real place, but reminiscent of times and places – it exists as a tangled web of references to past and future texts. This is the actual denunciation of history, creating a network of shared consciousness in which time flows in non-linear ways.

The first outstanding fact about it is that this model in modern literature was created by Jews in the late 18th century, and adopted ferociously by aspiring Jews like James Joyce and H. L. Borges in the 20th century. The second outstanding fact about it is that the writer who is considered the epitome of putting Jewish experience into modern literature was working against this tendency – Franz Kafka; his work is intentionally devoid of specific literary references. This is, for me, the deep expression of Jewish tragedy of the 20th century – becoming mute, speaking in a huge, empty space, stripped of echoes, of other people's voices.

I would love to hear your take on the issue of constant referencing, but also to ask about craft. It seems to me that retroactively I can always rationalise the chain of thought that led to writing a novel. But what about real time process: do you know from the start what path your characters will take? How do you go from a subject that bothers you to a character that enables you to examine it? How much freedom do you allow yourself as a writer? How much freedom do you expect to give?

Lavie

I think what I like is that when we talk, we can inevitably draw on a set of shared, obscure shaping texts. I have a very vivid memory of *The Einstein Intersection*, and I don't remember if we ever discussed it before, this book, so your mentioning of it, while seeming so natural, caught me by surprise.

I was backpacking across Europe. I was seventeen – I would turn eighteen a few months later, in Amsterdam. This was the early 1990s. I had gone to the army office and asked for permission to go travelling – I was supposed to join the army in the next few months, and no one quite accepted my own point of view, the selfish one, which was that I didn't really want to. It seems to me most of the Israeli speculative fiction writers made for poor soldiers. In any case, the person in charge asked how long I intended to go for and, unthinkingly, I said, "I don't know, six months, maybe?" He laughed in my face and gave me a slip of paper with permission to leave for a month. I took it, handed it over at border control, was allowed on my flight and promptly threw it away and forgot all about it. I finally came back, when the army began pestering my grandfather with phone calls, and I had already been backpacking for half a year… though I never did go to the army, in the end. I wish I could claim some sort of political high ground, but the sad, selfish truth is just that I didn't want to. Maybe if more people were selfish in just the right way…

But I'm digressing. I remember buying *The Einstein Intersection* in Budapest, in a second-hand bookshop. I think I still have the same copy, to this day. I read it while backpacking. I hitchhiked a ride from Budapest to Vienna, and from Vienna I hitchhiked to Venice. I was reading the book while tracing some of the same paths Delany took in the 60s, backwards.

There was something very strange, and liberating, in reading the Venice sections in Venice, a sort of cognitive dissonance, I suppose. The book itself describes a society which models itself entirely on referents, but imperfectly, since they do not have exact knowledge of the... can I say myth-images? – that they are imitating. And within that we have the story of the novel being written, as the author travels across Europe in the 60s, on the hippie trail.

The first – or maybe the fourth? It's hard to keep track – draft of *A Man Lies Dreaming* tried to do this. I was never actually very good at doing the author journal thing, but I loved the faux-authentic sections of the novel in which the author – 'me' – speaks. But they went in the edits, and I think it was the right decision, ultimately. I have an obsession with narrators, which maybe goes back to your question about craft. It's very important to me to always ask just *who* is telling the story. Which is the sort of question a historian must ask, I think. Because whoever narrates – even if we accept at face value that the 'narrator' is just a disembodied God-like 3rd person classic sort of narrator – there is still an 'I' telling the story. So who is it? What is their agenda? And this is something I think I took partially from *Kfor* – I knew it in theory for years, but in *Kfor* the question of the narrator takes a physical form, a practical form in the text. *Kfor* really had a big impact on me, in the literary sense, in the way that it reflected a lot of the things I didn't even *realise* I wanted to do with novels.

I experimented with this in *The Violent Century*, where it is not clear who the narrators are, a sort of disembodied 'we', though we get glimpses of them, from time to time. And, feeling more confident, I added a slew of narrators into *A Man Lies Dreaming*, only to realise I added too many, and had to cut a couple of them out. Now I'm trying something else again, which is to narrate three characters in three forms – in first, second and third person – but narrated by a single 'I'. I'm obsessed with form, with stricture, with limits. I'm obsessed with who is telling the story and why they are telling it. Most of my books I think take a very long time to gestate. *Osama* really started for me in 1998, with the American embassy bombings in Nairobi and Dar-es-Salaam – I was recovering from malaria in Dar-es-Salaam at the time and travelled up to Nairobi a week later, and by a strange twist of fate had stayed in the same hotel in Nairobi as the terrorists, only a little time before them. So it began there, and it grew, with other experiences, but it was only in 2008 that I sat down to write the novel – a decade later! – and only in 2005 I think that it first took early form in the shape of a short story, "My Travels with Al-Qaeda", and I knew I wanted to write more about those two people in that story.

I'm an instinctive short story writer. I can literally sit in front of a blank page with not a thought in mind and wake up hours later with a finished short story. You could give me a prompt and I'll sit down and do it. I did it the other night – I was asked for a story about some obscure theme, and I sat down late at night just to write a to-do list, just to make a note of needing to write something, and then two hours later I had written it. Don't ask me how that works! I only wish I could do it with novels.

I find novels hard. Short stories are my natural form. And with novels it's hard to get it right. I refuse to give up on them though; if it takes me years, I'll keep going back and try to get them right. At the moment it's my Palestine novel, which I've been trying to write and make notes for, for a very long time. It never quite worked, the shape of it, and I ended up – which I do quite often – combining several of the unsuccessful approaches together, and suddenly it took real form, it worked. A book that's had an impact on me is *The New York Trilogy*, which I admire but fail to like. I've been very interested in writing 'myself' as a character (though in fact I think Wolf in *A Man Lies Dreaming* comes closest to me!), so I'm writing Lior Tirosh into this book, but also the *other* Lior Tirosh – it's a book that's all about competing narratives, which is what the story of Israel is, for me. I'm just not sure anyone would care for it much, and to again, approach these themes with the ridiculous notions of pulp fiction – alternate histories and so on – I'm kind of resigned to a sort of obscurity by now. It doesn't actually bother me much – I am quite happy not to be invited to literary festivals or to give lectures, all those things you do – I like hiding away in remote places where no one knows or cares who I am or what I do. I've done my share of conventions and panels and book signings and literary evenings and so on, but on the whole I find it a bit of a drain. You seem to do a lot more of it than I do – do you actually enjoy it?

I don't usually know much about how the story would work, what path the characters would take – at most I can write a loose sort of synopsis that I can refer to, but I find a synopsis only really useful when I come to scripting a comic, which is quite a formally challenging experience, since you are bound by the number of pages, the position of the page, the number of frames… with *A Man Lies Dreaming* I knew the final line, though. In a way the whole book was written just to get to that final line, and it was – I can't even begin to tell you how satisfying it is when people react to the final line the way I *hoped* they would. When I wrote it, I thought it felt quite flat, I thought it wouldn't have any impact. Then I actually read the book, the first draft, and it just punched me out of nowhere when I got to it. I don't know how it works when you get something right. It just feels like magic.

But it's not, I suppose. I'm not one of the writers who talk about "my characters" and how unruly they are and how they're such darling little persons! But then writing for me is an exploration, so I just go along with whatever happens – sometimes it doesn't work, you write yourself into the wrong place and have to cut, cut, cut. I am the master of cutting by now. When I wrote *The Bookman*, it had a fun 16,000-word mini murder mystery in the middle, which had nothing to do with the plot, really. My agent told me to cut it and I did – I replaced it with a single sentence. He was right! It made no difference at all to the book. But I still liked it, so I polished it a bit and eventually sold it as a short story. I hate waste. The next book in that trilogy, *Camera Obscura*, was going along pretty well, then I began to notice the second part wasn't quite working, but I kept going anyway. Eventually I cut it all out – 45,000 words – and started again. This time it worked. I have entire novels I wrote that are sitting on the hard drive, finished but dead. All that endless writing, just for a few usable words...

But it's never wasted. Nothing is wasted. It just gets recycled, reworked, until you get it right.

I thought about your question some more, and it occurs to me that – for me – the key to unlocking a story, any story, always begins with a name. I'm obsessed with names – I spend a ridiculous amount of time on baby name web sites! – and until I find the right name for the character, I have nothing. So I think this is a truer answer to what you were asking.

But I'm sorry. I hate talking about 'writing'. It seems to me that everyone these days has a few novels out and suddenly they're offering writing advice all over the place, or speaking pompously of their 'process' or their 'craft'. It's not to say I don't think seriously about these things, but I don't find it very useful to suddenly set myself as an expert – I'm mostly aware of my own limitations, of the few things I can do passably well but of the many that I can't and wish I could. And of course, like many writers before me, or those in years to come, I too am beginning to look to academia as a possible hiding place, as a steady paycheque – and of course, what you have been doing in the past few years, very successfully I think, is teaching creative writing. So you must have had the opportunity to formulate, or formalise, a lot of your own thinking about the process of writing. Is that true? And also, we've argued in the past about how effective creative writing classes can really be. Surely writing must come from experience – that is, from life – but mainly from reading and writing, writing a lot, finding your own voice, learning from your mistakes. Writing seems to me a singularly solitary occupation. I know in America they love the shared experience, the "we talked about this", the *gibbush*, the social bond one forms in boot camp. In science fiction they have almost a cult with these, in particular with something called Clarion, which is a 6-week intensive boot (book?) camp for writers. I can't imagine anything worse, though for many people, I accept, it is an important, validating experience. How does this side of you – the teacher, the lecturer – how does it correspond with your writer side? Does it compliment it, or do you find it a challenge?

Shimon

Whenever I talk about writing, be it in a workshop or in a private conversation, I always get to the same claim – the best school for writing is reading other people's work. It's an unavoidable realisation, for anyone who teaches writing, it is a lesson worth learning. But what does it mean?

There are two kinds of reading, I think, a passive one and an active one. I spent many years being a passive reader of fiction. I read furiously, I read unto forgetfulness of myself. I didn't stop to contemplate how the ideas or the techniques employed were influencing me, how literary and genre conventions consoled me, brought me relief. I liked and disliked what I read. While in poetry I was analysing, tacitly, the poems I was reading, how things were done, why some lines had a ring of truth to them and others sounded fake, unappealing. I was studying, gathering knowledge; I was becoming myself by reading others' work critically. In fiction, my first instinct was to copy, not to distil principles and work them to suit my own voice. To turn my active reading on when I dealt with fiction was a labour, and that is what I wish for students in my workshops to be able to learn - not to be my students, but to shape their own way of becoming students. So it's important for me to take part in conferences and panels about writing, because I know that most of the Hebrew writers are passive readers of Israeli literature, which tends to be conservative in form and poor in technique.

One could say – techniques aren't needed in Israeli literature, the life in Israel is turbulent and eventful, you have so much content, dealing with form is redundant. I can't dismiss this so easily, if one sees the role of writers as social agents, who organise the raw materials of life in the minimal degree of order so they can be digested and engaged by readers. The danger of becoming an agent of the dominant ideology in the process never really scared off most writers in Israel: for them, it seems a fair cost for living within a community. I, on the other hand, have a fear of being devoured by the collective. Writing, as I said, is the only mean for me to con-stitute my autonomy, to gain some freedom. So being aware of what I do when writing, what others do, is essential. More so because you have to learn most of the time from writers who are foreign to Hebrew and Judaism, and the question becomes a practical one – how do I do it in Hebrew? How to make it as if the tradition of this kind of writing has always existed in Hebrew literature?

I can't pretend to be a pioneer. I hate the vanity typical of many works of the avant-garde. As if the fact that you are the first to do something has a value in itself. Because then one condemns his or her work to be conventional in time. What would have Edgar Allan Poe achieved just by writing the first armchair detective story ever? The heights of his writing are in stretching the limits of this form way beyond its imme-diate and strong formula in stories like *The Purloined Letter*, in which he offers a subtle and complex reflection on the meaning of acting out the role of the detective, the subject who is supposed to know, the messenger of Reason; or in a story like *The Man of the Crowd*, in which he's toying with his conventions in order to examine the concept of crime with which modernity is obsessed. T.S. Eliot, who I tend to dislike as a poet, said about Shakespeare that he has done the work of two poets in English, as an inventor of a new poetical lan-guage, and of figuring out the ways it functions in relation to his contemporary language. In Hebrew, the writer who singlehandedly naturalised most of the new forms, tropes and poetical devices of his time was Shmuel Yosef Agnon. He didn't do it as an innovator, but as a writer for whom all forms have always been at his disposal as a disciple of Jewish literature. But the act of naturalising never comes naturally. It's a struggle. You can see it in Agnon's work, you can trace the moments when he broke free, when he, in a way, became himself by becoming un-estranged to any form he liked.

How does one teach that? How can one learn that?

As an instructor of writing workshops I can only encourage students to experiment, I can only try to make them think about the craft. For me, the craft is not about adopting a series of rules – like, omit your adjectives and adverbs, refrain from explaining the motives of your characters and create scenes in which they are indirectly revealed, don't overcomplicate the plot, don't digress and so forth – all these are probably good bits of advice to better yourself as a writer, but they shouldn't turn into a manual of writing. The craft, for me, is asking after what you do while writing, what are the defaults and presuppositions, and finding methods for tackling them. I suggest to the students to look for the exceptions of the advice they get, and try to understand in what terms they work nonetheless, so they will know when to adopt them and when to put them aside. Let's say we discuss the importance of well-built and thought out characters. I would refer them to Kafka, who is really weak in creating autonomous characters, but is a genius in transferring the readers into the states of minds that haunt his characters.

I myself am a constant student. First I learned how to stop while reading, and never gorge myself on books. (There is a downside, though, I'm sated but never full, a thin layer of hunger is forever at the bottom of my reading. Sometimes it tires me down.) If a passage impacts me I let it linger and I try to reverse-engineer the effect (much like Poe, I guess...). I keep mental notes of techniques that impressed me.

My novel, *Undercities*, follows the life of Tiberias Assido, whose father is fascinated with an obscure Jewish mystic tradition. Every chapter is dedicated to another stage of her development, childhood, coming of age, etc. The whole depicts her growing to be a poet, and realising who she is in relation to the obscure mystic tradition that keeps appearing randomly in her experiences. She gets to a point in her adult life where she cannot adhere to any certainty anymore, and I discovered that my prose started to slip there – suddenly, in intense moments in her experience the style changed radically. For several passages, for instance, the prose becomes an elevated, stylish early 20th entury Hebrew prose and then drops; in other places it turns into fragments of a play, or very anal and controlled prose à la Hemingway and so forth. I knew right away where and when I learned how to do it, in reading Patrick White's *Riders in the Chariot*. I remembered how I was rereading this novel while studying how he used local changes of style to reflect changes in the mood of his characters. I used it differently, to suit my needs, but I picked the principle of freedom from his writing.

I put an effort into studying Faulkner's method of condensing two mechanisms of experiencing time into one consciousness in the story *The Old People*; taking it apart, internalising it, and finding a way to write it so it will reflect my own experience with the passage of time, its calamities, the gap between subjective time and the forms of experiencing time I was indoctrinated in as a religious child. I made a use of this study in *Kfor* and *Mox Nox*. (In different ways in each novel, but they are the fruits of the same study.)

I think I couldn't write anything in the past eight or so years without meditating about craft. In a way, my work *The Wedding Gifts* – which is composed of a couple of narratives, a long essay and sequences of poetry – is a meditation on craft. It starts with a conventional intent to tell a story, boring social realism to a point, and turns to the question of why I cannot maintain it, why the story is unable to live in these constraints that are the dominant model of Israeli literature. And the question of what kind of narrative, what style, what tone would be more adequate is then raised. The story restarts, with different modes of representation, with different attitudes toward the issue of how to give shape to consciousness in writing. The result is mirroring your work, and I'm quite certain that studying it sneaked in – it's a book about conflicting realities. In each of the narratives the main characters of the other narratives are invented, they exist as unreliable memories or figments of the imagination. They used to say that science fiction, in illustrating alternative realities, is a product of a postmodern sensibility and the loss of the concept of objective truth. Do you consider your work to be so? Do you think our generation is finding new ways for dealing with the assumption that there are only narratives and versions and cultural constructs? How do you engage with it?

Lavie

I don't think that at all – I don't think science fiction has had much use for postmodernism, but I don't think it had much use for modernism, either (and somewhat ironically). Both science fiction and fantasy must deal with the fact that their essence is ludicrous at heart. That is, it is imaginary, fanciful, fundamentally untrue. And yet it is something not seen before. It is something new. The idea of newness is fundamental to science fiction even as it has continually begun to digest itself over the decades, to become in itself a self-referential engine. But the argument goes that, in order to present the newness of science fiction (it's 'novum', to use a word I particularly dislike), you must resort to traditional storytelling techniques. You must seek to enmesh the reader in your made up world, convince them that the ludicrous and the impossible are real. You ask them to suspend their disbelief.

This is essentially incompatible with modernism, which seeks newness in form rather than content. And it is again incompatible with postmodernism, which seeks to always show off the essential ludicrousness of text and story itself, its artifice.

Science fiction must *convince*. This is not to say that elements of modernism or, later, postmodernism, haven't intruded into science fiction, because of course they have, but to this day I think its storytelling remains traditional at heart, and I also think that, for the most part, that may be the right way to do it.

However, I think what has bothered me most about science fiction in the past decade or so – that is, in the time of my own writing of science fiction, mostly in short fiction, which used to be the traditional way of writing SF – is that it has become so bloated with its own corpus that the new has rapidly devolved into cliché. What I mean to say is that science fiction is mostly in dialogue *with* science fiction. The word 'ghetto' is thrown about a lot when talking about SF (which has connotations I personally, for obvious reasons, find troubling), but it is true that for a large part it has – and continues to do so – been speaking – shouting – arguing – feuding – within its own walls. And the result of this is a set of protocols, of conventions, of *ideas*, that to a large extent were overtaken by the arrival of the future, too quickly. We cannot keep up with the world anymore.

And so – and I find this in my own SF, and the reason that, after finishing my last *Central Station* story at the end of 2013, I mostly stopped writing it – it now exists paradoxically only in relation to its past. The novum or novi are no longer new.

Terraforming and robots, faster than light spaceships and aliens, uploaded minds and artificial intelligences are all the staple diet of SF now, and most of them were around in the 50s (the only newish ones – to do with computing - date from the 1980s).

I am aware of this – my own writing constantly reflects and corresponds with older (though often more obscure) writers and stories. I can use new twists on them – my discarded Israeli soldiers, half-human and half-machine, speaking "Battle Yiddish" like the wind talkers of WW2, begging for spare parts on the streets of Tel Aviv or Jerusalem, for instance, are a case in point. I can even pinpoint the obscure references – specifically, in this case, two Hebrew stories published in *Fantasia 2000* in the 1980s, just as C.L. Moore's "Shambleau" is transformed in my *Central Station* stories into a "data vampire" – but the original story was published in 1933!

And I realised, after having been a prolific writer of these stories for a decade, that I have nothing new to add to science fiction. I believe there *are* writers who are genuinely seeking to engage with the newness of today. But I do not think I am one of them, and I think the majority of us seek comfort in recreating familiar fantasies, the sort of stuff we grew up on, just... upgraded a little. Sanded and polished and shined, but still basically the same.

And so I left it. And so, also, I had to ask – what is my aim? What is my purpose in writing?

My entry in *The Encyclopaedia of Science Fiction* contains one of my favourite ever sentences. It says: "[his] work can perhaps be most easily described in terms of Equipoisal Fantastika and Postmodernism, as his frequent use of Genre SF topoi is deliberately estranged".

I love this line because, on the one hand, it's a classic example of academic speak; and yet, at the same time, it makes perfect sense to me! I mean to say that it highlighted for me something that I perhaps did not fully articulate to myself. I use the tools – the topoi – of genre fiction in a postmodernist sense, that is true. I use them because I love them – because I find joy in them – but at the same time I see them as the box of old toys that they are. What is my purpose? And my purpose – certainly in that loose trilogy of the 20th century which includes *Osama*, *The Violent Century* and *A Man Lies Dreaming* – is to examine the shaping forces of that era, its violence and its political impulses, using a set of tools rarely designed for that purpose. It can be a frustrating experience – *The Violent Century*, for example, uses the idea of the Übermensch, the super-man, as its tool in talking about the century. Yet every review talks about it as "a superhero novel". That, to me, is missing the point. I don't care for superheroes. They are the tool – the silly, ridiculous tool! – that I use in that novel, but that novel is not *about* superheroes. It's a distinction that's hard to make when the only people likely to buy your book are the ones would do it solely in trying to replicate their own experience of reading superhero comics.

I don't *mind* – I use these tools out of affection, not contempt, and so I can't resent anyone for reading the novels for their surface value – but it can be a little tiring when it's the *only* thing people pick up on.

But I have to admit, what I choose to do *is* a ridiculous strategy. My agent often describes trying to sell my work as "trying to fit a square peg into a round hole". It is neither beast nor fowl. It's liminal, in the sense that it belongs neither entirely in genre nor in literature. I think when I am read – if I am read at all – it is mostly by science fiction fans. But so what? I am, inherently, a geek. Just maybe, sometimes, a self-hating one...

I should perhaps digress a little, incidentally, to say why I hate the idea of the novum so much. The critic Darko Suvin coined that term to refer to the essential core of the 'new' – the *idea* – at the heart of a science fiction story. Without that idea, that novum, Suvin argued, the story is not science fiction – that is, if the idea can be taken away, and the story still works – it's not SF!

To which I say – who the hell *cares*? Who *cares* if it's science fiction, or not science fiction? Kurt Vonnegut summed it up nicely, in an article he once wrote: "They love to stay up all night, arguing the question, 'What is science-fiction?' One might as usefully inquire, 'What are the Elks? And what is the Order of the Eastern Star?'"

To me, a story's a story. I do not care for taxonomy, this constant need to file things away into genres and sub-genres. I am proud of my *Central Station* stories partly because what I tried to do with them was to do away with this notion. I wanted to write slice-of-life stories – that just happen to take place in a weird, far-out future. I set them in Tel Aviv, in some undetermined time in the future. *No one* sets science fiction stories in Tel Aviv. And I wanted to simply write about relationships, and about family.

Science fiction, coming from the American pulps, has almost no notion of family. It has the lone hero, the cowboy. I wanted to write about what I know – the big, complicated familial network you and I know, the sets of obligations, the calendar of little things, weddings, funerals, bar-mitzvahs. And my practice with novums, in general, is to collect them, until I have a bunch – and then drop them casually into the background of my story, where they can do no harm. God save us from novums taking central stage! Science fiction is often described as 'the literature of ideas' – but who the hell wants to read endless ideas? Everyone has *ideas*. I wanted to write about the people who have to live with the consequences of all those ideas.

I like science fiction, I have to say, because 'realist' fiction seems to assume only the present – and only the present of the *author* – is valid. So forget science fiction as metaphor, for a moment. I want to read about life as it *might* actually be. In the last century we went from the telegraph to the Internet, from horse-drawn carriages to manned rockets to the moon and robots on Mars. You can't tell me all we can talk about is middle-aged men having an affair with their army secretary, or whatever. This stuff isn't even science fiction anymore! We have private spaceflight and Mars missions and augmented reality glasses. So how much *weirder* is life going to get in ten, twenty, thirty years' time? Let alone a hundred? I was asked about my definition of the future once at an event, and I said, that I think the future is where the familiar present stops, and things get weird. We can project our current reality, our present, a year, two years, three years into the future and we still know it. But then, at some point, there is a radical shift. Think of the difference between the 1990s and the 2000s. They're like two alien eras. The 1960s are as remote as the moon. Things get *weird*. And there's a joy in surfing that fracture line.

We like to say science fiction is a metaphor. It's literalising the metaphor. But sometimes, to paraphrase Freud, a Mars landing really *is* a Mars landing. And I love that science fiction, at its best, can wrestle with the big questions, the cosmic questions. Why are we here? How did we come to be? What else is out there, in this big, weird, mysterious universe of which we are but a tiny pinprick of light?

So this is how I am. I seesaw. One moment I love science fiction for what it can be, and the other, I hate it for what it is. Vonnegut again: "Along with the worst writing in America, they publish some of the best".

What drove me for a long time was that science fiction was essentially American. And, with the naivety of youth, I thought I'd storm that citadel. I'd make science fiction universal! No – I'll make it *Israeli*. I'll write about kibbutzim on Mars, and Yiddish speaking robots, and aliens who develop a symbiotic relationship with their human hosts – as their yarmulkes. I'll write science fiction set in Tel Aviv and fantasy set in Haifa and I'll show them, I'll show them all!

The crazy thing was, it actually worked. I don't know what anyone made of this stuff initially. Then, slowly, it began to be published, and published, and a decade later, I'm in magazines like *Analog* and *Asimov's*, and I have had at least one story, sometimes two, in every edition of *The Year's Best Science Fiction* for the past 7 years. That's mad! I'm this kid from a kibbutz who was reading translated science fiction in the adult library, in that dark little alcove between *Science Fiction* and *Crime*. What am I doing *here*? This isn't how it's supposed to happen!

And in 2008, I set out to be this guy who promoted international science fiction. I don't know what I was thinking. I managed to convince a small publisher in America, who published a lot of my early stuff, to let me do an anthology of international SF stories. I basically sold it on the concept that it won't sell 200 copies, but it would "look good". No one's done that – a few Anglophone writers did similar anthologies in the previous century, but it always came from that position of Anglophone dominance, their superiority. This was the first time someone from the outside, so to speak, was doing it. And it worked! We kind of hit a wave of interest. And I ran the blog that sprang up alongside it, for four years. They started giving me awards for it so I quit. But I'm still doing the anthologies – I've edited 3 so far, and am staying on as 'series editor' for more (which means I get to do all the paperwork but someone else has to read the stories – I just couldn't keep up, and it needed new, fresh eyes). And my new editor is from Pakistan! It's what I love about science fiction, how indifferent to borders it can be.

Editing is a bit of a hobby for me. I started with a weird little anthology called *A Dick & Jane Primer for Adults*, then I did the 3 *Apex Book of World SF* anthologies, and now I'm doing *Jews vs Zombies* and *Jews vs Aliens*, just because I *can*. It's a hobby, because I don't really make money out of it, and I'm not sure why I do it – mostly it's a headache. I wanted to ask you about that – you were a professional editor for six years, for a prestigious publisher in Israel – and you were their youngest ever editor, if I remember rightly. You worked on some very exciting books, including a lot of genre-friendly stuff. What is editing like, for you? Did you enjoy it? Do you find editing creative in its own right? I don't think we ever talked much about your editing days, and I'm genuinely curious to know more about that time in your life.

Shimon

My initial instinct is to put aside the questions about editing and suggest a slightly different angle on the science fiction issue. But I realise that: a) my recollection of my years as an editor is still painful and this would be just an avoidance tactic; and b) my take on the issue would be – I hope – more potent if I address the editing question first.

So, editing – I was offered a position as an editor in chief of the Hebrew literature department of a major publishing house at a young age. I was 28 years old and completely inexperienced. I was working on my thesis at Tel Aviv University, teaching there and writing on a weekly basis for a cultural supplement of one of the newspapers. I was an author of one poetry collection. The rock band I used to play in broke up after releasing one album. Not a rich, proven record.

But the times were changing in Israel. No, a paradigm shift was slowly taking place. For more than two decades the publishing scene was controlled by famous editors, who made a name for themselves during the 70s and 80s (back in the previous century – talk about the imagined future of sci-fi works arriving quicker than the consciousness can process its implications). The problem was that these editors had never really taken into account that they would grow old and detached from contemporary interest and being. They never thought about training the next generation of editors, never had any apprentices or interns.

In a way, one can argue that the blame for this delusion didn't lie with them, but with the literary atmosphere and the position of editors in Hebrew culture. Editors played a main role in orthodox Judaism (whenever I use the term 'orthodox Judaism', I hear my father's cry, "It's the only form of Judaism there is", and I have to quash it) at its formative stages: the ancients editors had the last say on what was to be canonical and what was to be discarded, turned to apocrypha, which books were to be included in the Tanach, for instance. Some of the inclusion and exclusion discussions are recorded in the Talmud and are fascinating. The Song of Solomon would have been deemed unworthy for its erotic nature had it not been for Rabbi Akiva arguing for its sake and pointing to the fact that the erotic streak can be read as an allegory for the union between the Virgin of Israel and God. The Book of Ezekeil had been feared for containing a dangerous mystical knowledge, the work of the Chariot and Hashmal (literally – electricity). A story about a boy who had become learned in Hashmal and has been consumed by fire is brought during the discussion. My novel *The Wedding Gifts* alludes to the two Talmudic discussions, maybe because it deals with canonical models of perceiving reality, or maybe because I'm still subconsciously vexed with my past as an editor. It's an irony that both the Mishna and Talmud, that report the editorial decisions as to the Tanach, were themselves edited by the most influential Rabbis of their times.

When Jewish culture sought to be reborn as a secular modern Hebrew culture, the editors once again became key figures in society. I'm talking about editors at large, who act in a double capacity: they are the gatekeepers of the literary cannon, and they are the ones who are doing the actual work of editing, namely, choosing texts for publication, cutting, rearranging, rewriting. This period – the end of the 19th century and the beginning of the 20th century – is often referred to, without any hue of cynicism, as the founding of the Hebrew Republic of Letters.

This ethos of editing as a way of maintaining the local Republic of Letters was kept nicely till the beginning of the current century. The editors were authoritative figures who decided the fate of new writers – in fact, for debut novels it was more important for critics and literary supplements who was the editor of the book than who was the writer. If a new novel came out, people would ask, "who edited it?" The name of the editor of a book is still mentioned at the credit pages at the beginning of each and every book published in Israel, and sometimes, in more old school presses, it appears on the back cover, with the editor's impressions of the contents.

It's not a bad thing altogether – I've been blessed in that manner that my editor in recent years is Yigal Schwartz, one of the last of the generation of gigantic editors. He edited my debut novel. Then we went on to our different paths. Eight years ago he called me and said that he wanted to publish everything I write, no matter how extreme and experimental my stuff is. It was liberating. I couldn't be more grateful for having an invitation to do my exploration into prose and poetry without having to think about the publishing end of things, knowing that I have a partner in crime, a reader whose only interest is the improvement of my writing, and who has no considerations of the commerciality of my work.

Yigal, who is also probably the most esteemed scholar of contemporary Hebrew literature nowadays, was a role model for me when I accepted the offer of the publishing house, because, you see, I did internalise the dominant ethos, and I thought that being an editor is first fighting over the nature of the literature written in Israel, its main trends and approaches to subject matter.

I did my own investigation, I read lot of contemporary literature, I analysed the main tendencies and forms and I knew right away, because of my personal taste and upbringing, what changes are required. As we discussed above, Hebrew literature is, at its core, a social or psychological one. At its best it's a realist literature, as its worst, a naturalistic literature. Yigal Schwartz was also hired at a young age, and his goal, as an editor, was to make way for experimental, multi-genre fiction alongside literature that addressed much silenced issues in Israeli society. He became the editor of Aharon Appelfeld, though he was much younger than Appelfeld. At the time,

Appelfeld was a lesser known writer, because his writing about the Holocaust, which was considered a non-Zionist and defeatist subject. (The irony! Since then the Holocaust has become the number one indoctrination tool in Israel, second only to racism.)

As for the non-realistic literature, Yigal's efforts to promote it were premature. The main reason was, I think, that real critical thinking in Israel was only seeping in. I believed that at the beginning of a new century, it should be a viable mean of expression of a younger generation of writers. Evidently, it wasn't a proclamation made from my newfound seat of power. On the contrary, it stemmed from a feeling that more and more talented writers sought new means of expressions that lay beyond the reach of the dominants models of Israeli literature, and I was granted the opportunity to bring their work to light. Those writers were exposed to Anglo-Saxon literature, cinema and comics; the tropes of speculative fiction were more immediate to them, as well as the workings of critical theory.

Carl Freedman claims in his marvellous book *Critical Theory and Science Fiction* that a chunk of science fiction works can be regarded as critical in essence due to the mere fact that they are a realisation of the maxims of critical thinking – every presupposition about our experience is just that, a presupposition and not a given axiom. It can be overturned and replaced. All our values are product of certain historical chains of events and they are contingent, not absolute. The works of Philip K. Dick, Ursula Le Guin, James Tiptree Jr., and Samuel R. Delany among others prove his claim.

But for me, speculative fiction, fiction that explores alternatives to the realities of the writers and readers, is all about the failure of the imagination. The verisimilitude it offers as fiction is nothing but a by-product, a platform for its incredible stunt - bumping against the boundaries of our ability to imagine.

The narrator of *The Wedding Gifts* defines himself as a science fiction writer, and at one point he says that he doesn't care if his speculations about future technology or science breakthroughs are convincing, as when he writes he explores the metaphors they serve. For him, he says, science fiction is about creating metaphors that are materialisations of mental structures. They are road marks in an endless search for adequate representational models for what he feels lies at the base of the communal consciousness of the society he is part of.

I guess this is my view as well. Every radical writer shows us how blind we are, how much we are bound by earthly existence, no matter how high we aspire to soar. Take Philip K. Dick, for example, he forces you to think about the rigid terms of perceiving reality as a given, he questions your sense of reality, but he is unable to think beyond the simple division of gender. For him, men are unquestionably male and women are obviously female. Take Ursula Le Guin, for her it's the other way around – gender is not a given, but the sense of reality is inborn, even in a work like *The Lathe of Heaven*, that deals with the line between dreams and reality.

Presenting the blind spots while exposing the way we take for granted other presuppositions of the human nature is the real critical act. At the beginning of the 21st century Israeli literature was ready for the shock of the critical act. A need rose for the introduction of new forms and themes. And even though I considered myself to be a mere conductive mean, and quite a replaceable one, I had only my experience to rely on.

Speculative fiction was for me the gateway to literature as a whole, as it was thanks to writers like Cordwainer Smith and Roger Zelazny in his best works, such as *Lord of Light* and *Creatures of Light and Darkness*, as well as the writers I just mentioned, that I got fascinated with rethinking forms, that I discovered the possibility of experimenting in style. Only later I learned that these writers were disciples of the great modernist movements and writers. I couldn't read Baudelaire and Whitman without reading Zelazny; I couldn't read Joyce without reading Delany and so on.

I disagree with your dismissal of the vital connection between SF and experimental writing. I chose for publication the works of writers who wished to examine the presuppositions of Israeli existence, or show by the failure to do so the blind spots of the examination. The work of Ofir Touche Gafla illustrated the need of young writers to produce new devices of fiction in Hebrew. Sayed Kashua just published his debut novel based on his experiences growing up as a secular Muslim Arab in Jewish-oriented Israeli society, and wished to find a new device to deal with conflicted identifications – with a westernised Arab-Israeli way of life and Palestinian identity – and turned to speculative fiction in *Let It Be Morning*. Einat Yakir's work was trying to apply the poetics of Yaacov Shabtai, a major writer who wrote with decadent prose about the life of the privileged stratum in Israel, to the life of marginalised populations and minorities. Shva Salhoub was formulating the experience of Mizrahi Jews in metaphysical terms. Nir Baram was rethinking life in Tel Aviv as life in which apocalyptic and journalistic description of reality got mixed up. Editing for me was first the effort to bring all these voices together and exhibit them as a new wave of writing. I regret not knowing you back then – your experiments in Hebrew with pulp fiction, like the merging of Lovecraftian themes in *The Tel Aviv Dossier*, which you co-authored with Nir Yaniv, would have been a great contribution to what I considered back than to be a fiasco.

I didn't realise how conservative most of the editors in the other presses still were. The books I published were attacked – no, the assault was on my approach and the books were just casualties. Some of the editors gave interviews questioning my method of editing – I claimed that the old method was (with, really, the exception of Yigal Schwartz) trying to fit diverse writing styles into the confinements of what is considered the recent trend in writing, be it literary Hebrew or spoken, loose Hebrew. My approach was to intensify the diversity and choose texts from the entire spectrum of writing with no apparent hierarchy of style. Others got more personal and when the novels I edited were nominated for awards or got prizes wrote to the papers letters or essays contesting the judges' decisions. It was ugly and aggressive, and one morning I woke up and realised I'm not that invested in the struggle, that any other young editor who cared enough for the state of Hebrew literature would do a better job than I did; that unbeknownst to me the sordid disagreements crossed the line between caring and ego-wars, and that my self-importance that was meagre to begin with wasn't worth preserving; that anyway we, who acted under the assumptions of the editorial Hebrew ethos, were all extinct; that a paradigm shift had occurred and the literary scene had become a buyers market, an industry, that the decision making as to the nature of Hebrew literature had moved into the hands of the readers and financial managers. So I left, sore but relieved.

It took a while to figure out that I learned one important lesson about the craft of writing and about what I seek in my own work through thinking in terms that were, I believed, foreign to writing. I was practicing the art of being attuned to other people voices, in order to strengthen them and make them more sound, and as a result I learned how to make my prose more flexible; I discovered my passion for human voices in writing.

What about you – you say you edit as a hobby, yet the world SF project must have clarified for you what you wish to do in writing. And what about different media? I know that you write comics and that you double as a screenwriter. In fact, I remember a period in which you were so obsessed with the adapting to comics an Israeli pulp series of novels that you couldn't write your fiction altogether. What are the relationships between these different kinds of writing?

Lavie

I don't think that editing influenced my writing in particular. What I was most affected by with the work on World SF was the realisation that I really wanted to follow my own path in writing, to use my own obsessions and background, rather than use someone else's. I'm pretty good at a kind of verisimilitude, in that I've lived in a lot of places and can make a passable – or even, let's say, acceptable – use of those locales. I can pretend to know more than I do, for the benefit of people who know even less. I wrote a bunch of stories set in South East Asia while I was living there, and people liked them, they sold, they got selected for Year's Best anthologies – but in hindsight, I am less than satisfied with them. They seem to me inherently dishonest. It was what eventually led me to the Central Station stories, which do borrow from that knowledge, that experience, but position it in a different, more honest and personal, context. I like editing the World SF anthologies because they give a voice to people, and in forming them I get to construct a sort of argument, about global literature and about science fiction. It might sound pompous, but at the same time, it's strangely idealist – it's not like I'm making any money from doing them...

What did begin to shape some of my writing is that my interest began to turn to comics, almost by accident. Someone asked me if I ever tried, I said no, and he said, why don't you? He had a magazine, and he had a pool of artists, and so I ended up writing my first comic strip without really knowing what I was doing. It was a terrible attempt at writing a script, but not, I think, a bad comic. But I find it fascinating. I find different mediums of writing fascinating. I branched into trying screenplays, more for my own curiosity (though I did have a couple of ill-fated screenwriting jobs, and the less we say about them the better!). In fiction you are God; you are the master of everything. Comics are a collaboration. There is an artist, and you are writing for that person. It's a visual medium; it's a different way of thinking. And with film, it's like stripping down a story as far as it would go. I love the minimalism of it.

I am interested in adaptation. That fascinates me. *The Violent Century* actually began as a screenplay. *Adler*, a graphic novel I have coming out, began as a screenplay. Sometimes I think a story is one medium, but it turns out to be another entirely. I was working on a novel last year. I knew it was good, but it also didn't *work*. And I didn't know why. It took me until recently to realise it was not meant to be a novel, but a comic; a graphic novel. I was thinking about it visually the whole time, I just didn't realise it. I wrote the script for the first issue, and immediately, it *worked*.

The problem with comics is it's so slow. You work with artists, and they have to carry a lot of the burden. I currently have 3 comics / graphic novels in development. I figure if I keep doing them, *eventually* one will be finished. You need patience. We never had comics when I was growing up in Israel, so I never really connected with it, and coming to it as an adult, I find a lot of it silly. But then you see the stuff that *can* be done with it, that *is* done with it, and it's an art form. It's wonderful. I would love to write more of it. Film to me is like putting down the skeleton of a story. It takes a world to make a film. Or you could take that skeleton and turn it into a novel, or a comic, and you don't need millions of dollars to do that!

The question is: do we see film or comics as any less an art form than prose? And the answer is, should be: of course not. They're just different ways of storytelling, and it's up to you to do it as well as you can.

I realised that I am very visually inspired, which I never really understood before. We talked about pulp a little, but I have to say, I never actually *read* much pulp. It's pretty bad, almost by definition. It took me years to realise that my fascination with pulp wasn't with the writing, the words, but with the pictures: the *covers*. And that's something I never understood!

I don't know what it was like for you – how did you get access to books? For me it was the library at first, on the kibbutz, but later it became the secondhand bookshops in Haifa, in the old Hadar area. It was a rundown sort of area, with cheap shops, shawarma stands, and a sort of treasure of used bookshops. My friend, Nir Yaniv, has exactly the same experience as me! He grew up nearby too. I'd go there whenever I could, it was about an hour away from the kibbutz, the big city! And I can't forget those shops. They lived on selling porn magazines that hung outside from strings, and translated Mills & Boon novels for a few shekels. But inside! Inside they had all the science fiction you could possibly want, and next to it, the Hebrew pulps. The Horror Series, Ringo the Gunslinger, Patrick Kim The Karate Man... you have to understand I never read these! I didn't know they weren't even really translated, most of them. They were what are called pseudo-translations; they were written by young Israeli writers for a bit of cash, who were sometimes credited as the "translators". They were ridiculous! But they had these amazing covers, most of which were by Israeli artists who specialised in these cheap pocketbook paperbacks. I only became seriously interested in them later; and reading about their history, that kind of informs my interest in pulps. When I was living in Jaffa, I don't know if you remember, I'd go through the flea market quite a lot, looking for them. And I'd find them sometimes, lying on a blanket on the ground, sold for next to nothing. I never knew Hebrew had produced so much pulp! Zionist romance chapbooks from the 1930s. Detective fiction. Erotica – Zionist erotica! And Westerns, horror, comics – comics in Israel were for kids, and I suspect it has a whole secret history, a vanishing history. There is so much, what I'd call marginal literature, which was never catalogued. It's inbetween the margins. It's not the stuff that got sent to the National Archives. So it's left to crazy old collectors to hunt for it or write about. There's a wonderful project in the U.S., the IsraPulp Collection, which attempts to catalogue some of this stuff. I have a couple of boxes myself. But it's fragile, it was never meant to last. It's non-canonical.

And I'm fascinated by that. Because it wasn't important literature, it was trash, it had a certain freedom, even a certain honesty, sometimes. I wrote a story, "The Projected Girl", which remains one of my favourites – one of the stories where I came closest to the ideal in my mind – and it's a sort of love song to marginalia, and the Haifa bookshops I remember, that entire world, which is mostly gone now.

So this goes back to your comment about my seeming obsession with this adaptation of a pulp series into comics. It was something iconic from my childhood, even if I'd never read it – and what I loved was the idea of taking an icon, a cultural signifier, and doing something new, something possibly interesting with it. But my obsessions usually have good reasons, I think. They're valuable to me in other ways than just money. For instance, in this case, even though I couldn't be involved, I ended up taking a few days to write my own version of it. A single-issue comic, in Hebrew, featuring Patrick Kim, the "two meter tall Korean-American secret agent", the "karate man"! And it required me to develop a system for writing comics in Hebrew! A way to format a script, even come up with sound effects! It made me laugh, a lot, and I did it, and then I moved on. It was a good experience, though. I learned something through doing it, and that's the only way you can become better, by trying new – sometimes ridiculous! – things. It had a lot of bad jokes in it. It was terrible, really, it was so camp. But it was funny!

One of the challenges was, what do I do with him, this man from the 1960s, a chain-smoker, what do I do with him in the 21st century? And I wrote this scene where he goes to see his boss, Colonel Hardy, and the colonel offers him a cigarette, and Patrick Kim extends his hand forcefully and says, "No! Even Patrick Kim has not killed as many people as cigarettes did!"

It's ridiculous, but I have to admit it was fun to do. Who knows, maybe they'll do it one day after all...

Humour, I think, is tremendously important. It's important to me, personally, in my writing, though my humour tends to be either full-on slapstick (like in some of my short stories, or my Hebrew novel with Nir Yaniv, *Retzach Bidyoni* (*A Fictional Murder*)), or it tends to be very dark. *A Man Lies Dreaming*, I think, is essentially a comedy. The circumcision scene... that makes me laugh. It's so awful, but it makes me laugh. The thing about the Holocaust, even as it was happening, was that people made jokes. They used humour to try to cope.

A Jewish friend told me a joke the other day and I laughed. She asked me what was worse than having a fly in your soup. I said, I don't know, what? She said, the Holocaust.

You have to laugh. I don't know if you could laugh at this if you're not Jewish. But you have to laugh. The humour is protection; it's a way of coping with horror. A South African friend of mine wrote crime books about Apartheid, and they are uniformly dark. I can never read them. And I said, you have to stop; you have to take a break inbetween the darkness. I call it the Enid Blyton Principle. You need to stop and have a picnic, lashings of ginger beer, whatever it was the Famous Five did. There has to be light. It makes the darkness all the more terrible, when it's set against the light, but it's also hope. My novels are generally about light. Fogg walks into the light at the end of *The Violent Century*. Joe in *Osama* turns away from the light. This is what the choice always comes down to.

Humour, I think, is essentially subversive. Humour is political. And I think one of the things we keep going back to, part of the problem in the political conversation in Israel, is the lack of critical humour. One of my inspirations, I think, was the 1990s sketch show, Ha'chamishia Ha'kamerit (The Cameri Quintet), which had writers like Etgar Keret and Asaf Tzipor. It was incredibly subversive. It was political. It was very funny. They addressed racism and the occupation, and the Holocaust, sexism, the myths of Zionism – but they were funny, and pointed, and they were *needed*, it feels to me. The clown is the one person in the court who can speak the truth without being punished for it. Whereas today, I don't think we have that. I think mostly, humour in Israel now serves the status quo. I think of Eretz Nehederet (A Wonderful Country), which is supposedly a satirical show. It's painful to watch. It's humour that's on the side of the strong. It's bullies' humour.

What guides me, I think, as a writer, is a pretty simple principle. You should always be on the side of the weak. You should challenge the ruling narrative. It's not always easy. It's not a path covered in glory, and no one throws hundred dollar bills at you as you walk it. But it's right.

The problem is, I have no talent for art, and no talent for music. I have no talent for a great number of things! Music for me is a constant background for writing, but it tends to be just that – background. Whereas for you, I think, music plays a much more important role. You have written lyrics for some of Israel's leading musicians, and similarly, your poems have been set to music. You were in a band, you still play every week, if I remember right, and just recently some of the biggest names in Israeli music hosted a special evening dedicated to your songs. I am honestly fascinated. What is your relationship to music? How do music and words intertwine? Do you 'hear' music the way you hear words, when you compose music? Your first novel is set in the rock scene in 1990s Tel Aviv – did you ever want to become a rock star yourself?

Shimon

A rock star? Never. But I would often daydream during my early twenties about becoming an 80s alternative new wave star. A Robert Smith after releasing *Pornography*, a David Sylvian in his post-Japan phase, a Mark Hollis, a Nick Cave, a Patty Smith, or if to stay local – Rami Fortis and Barry Sakharof in Minimal Compact. They all seem to be some sort of absolute artist, for whom all aspects of art – both creating musical poetry and performing it – were an extension of individuality; they were consumed by self-expression.

Of course this view had more to do more with my adolescent imagination (I am a late bloomer. Hopefully I have yet to reach my peak...) and less with the reality of things. It's very easy to get confused as to what you are passionate about. My passion and my need for a devotion mixed two separate motivations: a banal and circumstantial one with a true and deep one.

The irrelevant one was evidently the exhibitionist side of art. I was in a rock band, I thought that I'd like to be on stage and perform, I wanted my personality to shine and radiate, to reach others. I didn't stop to think what this personality is and what is so unique about my youthful angst and morbid fascinations that can evoke anything in other people. Maybe I thought it would appear in the process, that I'd become someone worth seeing by the sheer insistence of waiting to be seen. But I think the real reason was that I already had a model in my head against which I was working.

I already talked about studying with my father and about learning holy scriptures by heart. The studying, which had been intimate, also had a public aspect. I was a quiz kid, I've been sent to myriad quizzes revolving around Jewish subjects – Bible quizzes, Jewish lore and laws quizzes. And I won; I would get the first prize in almost every contest. I remember, shamefully enough, a quiz in which I came in second place, and my father refused to believe it. My score was so ahead of the other participants, that the final round, in which all three last contenders had to answer an identical question in writing, was insubstantial. When the results were announced, my father got furious. He started a fight with the judges, demanding to see the answers in writing. I think that's when I decided that I couldn't take it anymore, that I had to stop taking part in these quizzes. Anyway, my winnings almost always got me beaten up by other kids. There were two rival elementary schools in my hometown. The kids from the other school would taunt me whenever they saw me on the street, on my way to the public library, by myself. They would have hit me, had it not been for my older brother, who was infamous for his strength and his friendship with their schools bullies. Saved by the alliance of bullies, there's an idea for a comics.

But I guess I didn't get over the stage fever, yet I wanted to be on stage on my own terms, not reciting knowledge, but doing my own thing, being totally myself. I learned to play the guitar by myself, just the basic chords and scales from a book. And once, when I was on my way home during my army service, and trying to catch a ride at a junction not far from my hometown, a friend of my cousin's stopped for me. We talked and he told me that my cousin told him I was writing poetry and maybe I'd like to show him some texts. He was starting a band and he was looking for someone to write the lyrics. He said, "you know, like The Smiths".

It was a weird coincidence, we both took as a sign – I was at the time obsessed with *The Queen is Dead* and was listening to it repeatedly on my walkman (walkman, for crying out loud, cassettes!). So we agreed that I'd write him some texts and he would give me guitar lessons. Not a long time passed before I joined his band as a second guitar player.

It wasn't unusual to join a band in Sderot at the beginning of the 90s. No special playing skills were required, just a desire and some musical instincts. Sderot exploded with young artists – all of them the children of North African immigrants, all of them seeking a way to give a meaning to growing up in a forsaken town, to a silenced population: there were musicians and filmmakers, writers and thinkers. It was a scene bursting with talent and the desire – so much borrowed from existential philosophy - to have an authentic voice, to be *sui generis*. I was getting acquainted with the scene and was amazed. Everybody in it read Albert Camus, held a copy of *The Stranger* and *The Myth of Sisyphus*.

Then when my band moved to Tel Aviv, I got my chance to perform and realised I hated it. Standing, midway through playing our songs, I was thinking what the line-up was and when the concert would be over. I couldn't get into it; there was a gap between composing the songs and performing them. We recorded our first album and broke up. I had the same experience with poetry readings. The words would sound hollow in my mouth, devoid of all the potential energy rustling in them when putting them down on paper. I drew away from public readings.

Sometime it takes a while to figure out that things are made of separate elements, and that our reaction is often to the organisation of the elements, to the interaction between them, and not to the elements themselves. We place too much emphasis on our distain of one element when what really raises the feeling of aversion in us is the context in which it is presented.

For a long period I kept my poetry unconnected to my music, because of the affinity between poems and lyrics (in Hebrew, it's the same word for poem and song). I was convinced that in poetry the words carry their inner music and it's shown on the page, in the alliterations, punctuation, cesuras, blank spaces, the emptiness surrounding the texts.

While in songs, the text is lacking without the music, the way a human voice invokes it. My experiments with music became isolated. I would write songs on my guitar and record them, leaving them on my hard drive.

In my second collection of poetry, *That Which I Thought Shadow is the Real Body*, I tried a different approach to writing. I began with a question. Throughout my first collection of poetry I was trying to piece together my past and identity by turning to the frameworks that gave them meaning – history, mythology, tradition (well, modernity is all about understanding the self via various temporal mechanisms). I asked myself, what if I'm to strip my writing of these frameworks, wouldn't I get to very essence of poetry, the way the words work naked of imposed meanings, through their pure sonic qualities?

It was a failure, but an indispensable failure. The very thing I was looking for was missing – the voice. I searched for this aspect, how it can be brought back. At that time I worked at a friend's studio, we were writing an album for another friend – I wrote the lyrics, and Kobi Oz (who is a household name in popular music in Israel) was composing. Kobi asked me to record something for a collection of artists in his label. The studio was empty at nights for a week, and he told me I could have it for the period if I wanted. There were two other guys that worked there as well – David, a sound assistant who is an accomplished musician and Shimon, who was the studio's leading sound engineer. We spoke during the days of recording and agreed to stay at night and experiment. I told them about the difficulty with my manuscript that I was facing, and David asked if I had tried bringing back the voice in the simplest manner, by performing the poems.

We did a couple of trials. First we tried to compose one of the poems. Composing poetry is very common in Israel. Most of the local musicians compose with known poets. (Therefrom stemmed my wish to separate my poetry from my music. I like many of the compositions. *Good Wine*, by Ilan Virtzberg and Shimon Gelbetz, an album based solely on the poetry of Yona Wallach, is a masterpiece. But somehow, once a poem becomes a song, its music is set, you cannot phrase it to yourself any other way, you cannot interpret it without hearing the singer's voice in your head.) It didn't work. We tried to perform them as spoken words, writing a basic beat, and letting the words carry the weight of the poem. It didn't work.

At last, David came up with a harmony on his guitar that was inspired by one of the poems and Shimon suggested to record it. Then he said, "get into the recording room, I'm opening a microphone, just read the poem with it, play with it".

That was that – it came to me so naturally, I knew right away when to flow with the guitar and when to contradict the harmony with my reading, how the words – sound and meaning – interacted with the music. We didn't just find a solution for a poem, we discovered we could make an album of sorts, creating musical versions of the poems (the album came out as part of the collection of poetry). And I understood that I had been judging my interest in music through the performing lens, but the foundations of music – rhythm, beats, tempo, sound – were what intrigued and fascinated me, their becoming vibrations of air, the marks they left on the body.

I began thinking about ways to bring together my experience in music and in writing. I sought other musicians with which to collaborate in poetry performing projects. Usually I'd work with musicians for a short period, we'd perform and be done with it.

On the other hand I embarked on an investigation: how to incorporate live music into writing. It was natural to me, in writing fiction, to make it into a subject, and *One Mile and Two Days Before Sunset* is a novel set in the 90s music scene in Israel, though the scene is not the main interest of the novel. But I invented, while writing it, an alternative rock group named *Blasée et Sans Lumiere*, and a legendary singer-song-writer, whose songs I wrote as well, and I had to find ways to describe music in words, so the description would transmit the sense of music the group were doing. Not that before-hand I didn't have the need to describe music, but as many other poets I have shortcuts; I'm synesthetic to a certain extent, I'm quite skilled in making metaphors for one sensory impression using another. Here, I had to adhere just to music, to follow the manner in which it impacts on the auditory system, the ways it invokes in one's psyche metaphors for capturing its fleeting essence.

Since then I can only write if I first define my relation with music to whatever demands to be written. *Sunburnt Faces* was written with music serving as a divination tool. I listened to music, mainly American indie music, till I fixated on one song and then used the picture the song raised in my mind as the central scene for the chapter I was writing. I just came off translating Philip K. Dick's *The Man in the Hight Castle* into Hebrew, so I wasn't very original. He used the I-Ching as a tool to decide the development of his novel.

My third collection of poetry was born out of music. As I said before, I was mourning, language was damaged, broken, unstable. Every form of poetry was unreliable. It got infected when I used it. I had to, with each new poem, redefine the form, so I clung to music. The collection itself is totally measured, you can read it with a metronome, yet every poem has an independent inner tempo and metre that produce a different musicality. I had to pull my speech from the abyss of the ineffable by first turning to the amorphic nature of music on the one hand, to the stubborn basis of the beat, on the other. *Mox Nox* was written by also clinging to a beat, to the heartbeat of the narrator. My father had a stroke, I was visiting him in the hospital and came back exhausted – I fell asleep, a short, heavy sleep. I woke up with a foreign heartbeat in my ears. I kept it all along the writing, its changes with the changes in moods, always rhythmic, but never fully mechanical. I twisted the syntax; I used rare forms of words, just to fit the narrative into the beat.

It is strange to hear people saying that comedy is about timing. For me, writing, in its manifold forms, is about timing, about portioning and encapsulating time, managing time. Or at least about the effort to do so. And attending to language as music is a way to structure time. Comedy resides elsewhere, as far as I can judge. I have a slim sense of humour, few things make me laugh. I find children to be funny. Mainly their efforts to understand the world, to systemise it, that concludes in greater misunderstandings.

Or, if to generalise it more, unawareness is a funny thing when it comes shrouded with certainty, when there is a deep uninformed gap between one's claims about reality and the facts. The funniest sketch I remember from The Cameri Quintet was a monologue of a yuppie woman about waking one morning and discovering there is such thing as the Palestinians, an ethnic group of people under the Israeli regime, who suffer. She addressed the camera, totally shocked by the discovery. It was the mid-90s.

Another sketch, more recent, that works in the same manner, is at the opening of a new satirical show, *The Jews are*

Coming. A family is eating dinner, and complaining about the day they had and the nuisances they suffered at work. Whenever a family member is done with complaining – about the greed of the banks, about a girlfriend, about a new child in the family's mother's kindergarten – the other members of the family say, you should murder them, I would have murdered them long ago. Slowly you understand they are the Amir family. But when the younger son asks, "what do you say about this guy, Rabin?" The father says, "Yigal, I beg you, no talking about politics at dinner!"

(Yigal Amir is, of course, the man who assassinated Prime Minister Yitzhak Rabin in 1995.)

The exposure of the confident obliviousness of some milieus is evidently political. That is the reason I don't like the American shows that are smug about it, like *Curb Your Enthusiasm*, in which Larry David is celebrating the notion of his narcissistic ignorance of others. When one turns aware of his unawareness and boasts about it, I tend to be disgusted, not amused.

Things get hilarious for me when they verge on the absurd and the nonsensical. Absurdity and nonsense don't undercut the critical momentum. On the contrary, if they are done properly they can show the dangers of maintaining innocence. Maybe because I grew bitter as a person I see no more how innocence, even child-like or religious, prevails in this world without becoming a form of corruption.

While writing this down I suddenly understand that the concept of innocence as corruption underlines many of my works, and in particular *Sunburnt Faces*. The first part of the novel is about Ori's innocence clashing with reality through the divine call she hears. She reads the books of the prophets in order to understand the meaning of God's message, the role she was entrusted with. She misreads them. She thinks she should punish her ex-best friend for her sins of betrayal, to cleanse her from the corruption of sin, and electrocutes her. To her best understanding, Hashmal, electricity, is the true cleansing agent. I was laughing when I wrote the passages. Not many readers found it funny, though. Most of the reactions I got were as to the cruelty of Ori's actions led by her misinterpretations of the scriptures. I wasn't aiming at a social commentary with that. I was interested, as I said earlier, in the relationship between childhood, religious experience and the modern notion of Wonderland. When Ori, as an adult, contemplates this relationship, she has to confront language, or the boundaries of human expression. Expression is always pushed into linguistic paradoxes when trying to illustrate a state of transcendence; it employs contradictions and nonsense. You can reverse engineer this process, start with nonsense and follow it back to its origin, the passion to regain innocence in a world where innocence demands silencing some voice, some existence.

Another thought that occurs to me now is about the age old connections between catastrophe and humour, between horror and the religious experience, or faith. You talked about the Holocaust and humour, but what about religion and faith? Your collection of poetry is called *Remnants of God*, and in your early works, like *Occupation of Angels*, you dealt with theological themes, but we never discussed the role of religion and faith in your life and their affect on your writing. Does it bother you? Do you consider your work to be secular? Can one have a secular faith?

Lavie

I think you're wrong about *Curb Your Enthusiasm*, though. 'Larry David' in the show is a construct, a send-up of himself,

99

the clown who is allowed to say the unspeakable and get away with it. Perhaps you don't like it since it's too close to what you yourself describe about your work. He's childhood's innocent, who can point and ask the questions the grownups can't, to point out the king isn't wearing any clothes, so to speak. Though we can always agree to disagree... What I find quite arresting is when you describe Sderot and that energy – and of course many of your contemporaries went on to become successful musicians, actors, authors. It's striking to me because it was the opposite for me, and this is a problem that has bothered me for a long time. I think kibbutz life, its underlying principle, was to aim for a sort of comfortable mediocrity. You didn't want to stand out; you didn't want to challenge the system. It was very conformist. And I note we produced a lot of generals, and a fair amount of businessmen, but not so very many artists. I also envy you your relationship to music, which, like faith, is something I mostly lack.

The truth is that I'm fascinated by faith, which is something I seem unable to experience. I know I grew up in a secular environment, but many people find faith later on in life (or, in the other direction, fall out of faith, as you did). My father seems to have become a lot more religious later in life. And he likes to tell the story that I came back from kindergarten once and declared: "There is no God!" He asked me how I knew and I said, with utter confidence, "Because the teacher said so!"

So I wonder. Is that all it takes? Upbringing? I know many people search for meaning, but I don't think I ever did. When I was younger I travelled a lot, I backpacked, I smoked a lot of weed, wrote poetry, grew dreadlocks (for a long time – all gone now, alas. Age catches up to us all...). And my parents always "accused" me – it always sounded like an accusation, at least! – that I was "searching for myself". But do you know, I never did! I don't think that I did. I just liked backpacking, and I liked getting stoned on the beach... I think it was great! It certainly beat going to the army for three years. I had a great time. And I was working towards being a writer, by doing the best thing you can – simply living, experiencing things.

So I never had religion. I have a sense of how weird the universe is – how mysterious and strange it all is – it's not something I can understand. It's too big. It's beyond our scope. But I have little interest, weirdly, in any type of creator. After all, as children we rebel against our parents, so if there were a God – especially of the rules and punishment kind – my instinct would immediately be to be on the side of the rebels. You know what Blake said about Milton, that he was "of the devil's party without knowing it". Milton wrote so much more beautifully of the fallen angels. I like Blake. He is one of my favourite poets, following his own weird vision. Though we need to distinguish, I suppose, between faith, which is belief, and religion, which is a system. I am not that interested in religion, but I am fascinated by faith. Why do some people experience it, and others don't? It strikes me that it would be absolutely wonderful to *have* faith, to experience it. It must be a great comfort. To not have it is to experience "Aubade", the Larkin poem. The "total emptiness" he writes about, but writes about clear-eyed and so, so beautifully. How can life not have a meaning, and yet everything comes together to produce something as haunting as "Aubade"?

I come closest to believing when I cook. Cooking strikes me as such an unlikely thing! Take something simple: a fried egg on a slice of toast (very English!). The egg comes from a chicken, cooked in butter made from the milk of a completely different species (or oil made out of plants, a completely different kingdom), and then the bread! Yet another plant, treated in a complex process, and mixed with bacteria, all to produce... breakfast. It's remarkable. The complex interconnectedness of human food is only more surprising by how powerful it is on our senses, how *good* it can be. Finding God in food. That's something I'd like to find a way to write about.

What I never realised, until someone actually pointed it out to me, was that the motif of faith as a form of addiction keeps repeating in my work. I honestly did not realise this, but from the very early story that serves as the basis for most of the science fictional universe I've spent years developing, this is present. In "Crucifixation" I have cyborgs in a future Israel, who now beg for spare parts on the streets of Jerusalem, and only look to score the drug of the title, which allows them a momentary release, a religious experience. I more consciously returned to that story, and updated it somewhat, in "Robotnik", which is part of my Central Station cycle, but that theme is everywhere in my fiction (it's central to Gorel, for instance). Of course, in SF you can literalise the metaphor, which I guess is what I subconsciously did. Why that should be I don't know. I do think that there is a need to write about the really big questions: Why are we here? That's a big question, isn't it? I'm fascinated by the universe being seemingly 'fine-tuned' for human life. But could we not just be a mere side product? We still know so little about the universe. What is dark matter? What came before the Big Bang? We can only think in terms of the time/space continuum we exist in, but 'time' itself did not exist before. Are there other worlds, other universes? I want to write about the human experience, yes, but at the same time I recognise how limited that is, because the universe is so much bigger and so much stranger than we are. Science fiction allows you the possibility of that. Of talking about the big questions, there is a novel I have been trying to write for a long time – not exactly science fiction, and yet about that question, of why are we here. Why the universe. I am still trying to write it now. There must be a way for us to discuss the world beyond ourselves, beyond being human. But it's a hard act. And we need to still put it into patterns we understand, and can relate to – stories, and stories that are about people. And it's hard not to make it banal, too. We can't offer answers, after all. Prime numbers fascinate me. They're very strange. Like cooking, they seem to me to offer some sort of clue as to the nature of the world. And of course, I am very much influenced by Philip K. Dick, whose view of reality in his fiction was always incredibly malleable, ductile. I spoke to friends of his, who told me he would constantly come up with new ideas, new beliefs. "I've woken up this morning and found the true meaning of life!", and he'd tell you all about it. And then the next day, you'd ask him and he'd say, "No, I was totally wrong! Now *this* is the *real* explanation!"

And I think he took great delight in it. He did have a real religious experience, and he was so affected by it that he spent the last ten years of his life trying to understand it. And it's that experience that I find so fascinating. Did you know you can stimulate it using technology? There is a device that uses magnetic fields on the brain to induce a religious experience. I'd love to try it, but they don't sell it for self-assembly at Ikea…

I think, with *A Man Lies Dreaming*, I hit a certain point, where I finally wrote something I was almost entirely happy with. It seemed to me to say something I needed to say, and say it as well as I could. So in a way, I feel less pressure – on myself – to continue, to push. But having said that, I still feel

I have things I want to say, big themes I want to explore. The question of Israel and Palestine and competing histories, warring histories, is one. The question of God, of why are we here, is another. That's two novels I've been trying to write for a long time. I hope I manage them.

You mention your realisation that what you thought you wanted turned out not to be the thing you wanted. I'm finding it too, I think. I do not like to perform. I find the public life of being 'an author' exhausting. My instinct is to withdraw. So I want to take you back to the start, Shimon. I started full of doubts, and I think I leave this conversation with renewed energy, willing to have another go at railing at the world. We're doing this book... let me ask you this, as our final question: do you not think this is just hubris? There is a kind of ego you need, as a writer – both an immense belief in yourself, in how special you are, and what truths you alone can impart to the world – and it's coupled with a constant self-doubt, an awareness that you are *not* special, that at best you are just another writer amongst a myriad others, all shouting into the void... I became a writer because I wanted to change the world, now I realise sometimes I can barely change my shirt to get a clean one.

Do you think it's all worthwhile?

Shimon

Why does the last question have to be the hardest? It's not that you save it to the final moment; it is because it becomes clearer and clearer that you are forever condemned to return to a starting point, seeing it with fresh eyes. Can one overcome it? Nietzsche asked the question in the most ferocious manner, and I believe he is adamant in his argument – you have to, if you are to carry your humanity with pride. It is a mission to be human, to have a self, and yet, one never gets to choose, one is never asked if they are willing.

Hassidic Jews often quote Rabbi Meshulam Zusha of Hanipol on the matter. He used to say, "When I stand before the Maker and He asks me why weren't I Moses, I'll know what to answer. But when He asks me, 'why weren't you Zusha', what answer will I give him?"

So we skip epitaphs and last meals and rush to the Heavenly Court – what do we have to say for ourselves? What name do we give when a voice finally answers from the void and demands to know who shouts out there?

You have the answers you need. Writing – be it writing speculative fiction or detective fiction or poetry or your unique mesh of them – enables you to stay in contact with the initial awe and bewilderment we slowly forget as we go along. So, it might not be a question of worth, but a question of necessity for both of us. I share with you that principle, but apply it somewhat differently. I have to become better at being myself. The meaning, the purpose, comes second, after understanding the method – how to become better. I won't improve in the art of becoming myself unless I re-imagine this self into more vibrant forms of existence, full of radiance.

PART TWO

War and Art

The following two stories were written in the summer
of 2014. Following the abduction and murder of three
Israeli teenagers in June, a Palestinian teenager,
Mohammed Abu Khdeir, was kidnapped in retaliation
and set on fire; two of his murderers were similarly
underage. On the 8th of June the Israeli army began an
intense rocket bombardment of Gaza, followed by a
ground assault, in response to Palestinian rockets fired
towards Israel. The operation led to the death of over
2000 Palestinians, and 72 Israelis.

Both of the stories here are haunted by the image of the
burning boy; both struggle with the futility of poetry.
They, too, represent a conversation; and each author
appears as an aside in the other's story.

Tutim

LAVIE TIDHAR

In the middle of the night the telephone rang. Lior Tirosh picked up the phone and a voice said, "Run."

Tirosh stared blearily at the ceiling. A black cloud of mould had spread gradually over one corner of the room. It had began as a mere speck of dirt, some long while back, but now it had extruded aggressively outwards, had colonised and settled and stayed. The last time he'd spoken to his landlord, Yossi, the man had told him to use hot soapy water to gently wash off the mould. But Tirosh never did. In many ways he was a lazy man, not given to undue intervention in the little injustices of life. It was easier to let the mould grow than to try and combat its spread, knowing that anyway it would just come back, that one day, whatever he did, the mould would grow to cover the entire flat and, later, extrude farther, until first the city and then the entire Syrian-African Rift Valley would come under its sway. In such a world, Tirosh thought, still, perhaps, in that uncanny valley between wakefulness and dream (for he was usually a deep, if late, sleeper), the mould would eventually develop intelligence, and with it a sort of symbiotic relationship with the humans, whom it would enslave. In such a world (now so vivid in Tirosh's mind that, for a moment, he all but forgot the strange telephone call he was in the midst of), a person would be marked from birth with the Black Sign of the fungus, perhaps on the forehead or – like the small round scar of a smallpox vaccine – on the arm, close to the shoulder. The Pax Fungi would then herald a never-before-seen era of peace and prosperity across the Middle East and beyond, until it extended across the entire planet. It would be a golden age never before seen in human history, and would – "Are you listening to me, Tirosh?" the voice demanded.

Outside, Tirosh could hear the creaking, halting sounds of a street sweeper as it crept along Hatkuma Street, which is to say, the Resurrection, right up to the intersection with Hatchiya, which is to say, Rebirth Street.

This was not out of the ordinary. Tirosh had first moved to Tel Aviv from the periphery. He had grown up on a kibbutz up north, a lonely child immersed in books for too long a time for his own benefit, like a Catholic child baptised forever in cold, if holy, water. Back then, he lived for a time in an apartment which sat on a confluence of streets all named for ancient pogroms. Blood libels and dead Jews haunted him on trips to the greengrocers and the local kiosk until, at last, he'd fled, past countless peeling Bauhaus contraptions that littered the sandy grounds of Tel Aviv like candy wrappers or empty, discarded packs of cigarettes, south to Jaffa.

"Who is this?" he said, sleepily.

"You have to leave," the voice said. "They're coming for you now."

Tirosh sat up, suddenly awake.

"It is no longer safe for you there," the voice said. "Go. Take nothing with you."

"Not even poems?" Tirosh said.

"You don't understand," the voice said. "They are coming for all the poets."

He – it was a man, with the slightly hoarse voice of a smoker – halted on the line. Behind him Tirosh heard the screeching of police sirens passing nearby, and a man shouting, and the sudden, startling sound of breaking glass.

"Run," the voice said, again, and then the line died and took him with it.

Tirosh stared into the darkness. So it had come to this, he thought, chilled. He got up without turning on the lights. He dressed quickly, in dark jeans, and running shoes, and a faded, ancient T-shirt from the Witches concert at the Arad Festival in '94, which was a year before the festival was shut down following the death of two girls and a boy, who were crushed to death in the crowd during a Mashina concert, and three years before the death of the Witches singer herself, Inbal Perlmuter, in a car accident. Tirosh had been mildly in love with Perlmuter at the time, though from a safe, platonic distance. Now he picked up the bag he had had waiting, prepared, by the bedside. It contained what little cash he had, a change of clothes, phone tokens, a copy of his first published collection of poetry, *Remnants of God*, and a copy of the single issue of the magazine he'd edited with Shimon Adaf, *Echo*, before Adaf was taken to one of the concentration camps they had built in the Galilee to house writers of the fantastic. He also packed three pens, a blank notebook, and the completed manuscript of the book he'd been working on for the past two and a half years, *The Death of Hebrew Poetry*.

When he peered out through the blinds he saw an unmarked car slide silently into a parking bay across the street and three men come out. They wore civilian clothes and moved swiftly and efficiently across the road, not hurrying, and he even thought he recognised one of them, a minor literary critic, or so he had styled himself back in the day, a *mevaker*, which could mean critic or visitor, and Tirosh would say, savagely, that the man was only a visitor to literature, not even that, someone who stood far away and looked out to literature and did not know it, like Moses at the summit of Mount Nevo, looking over the promised land which had been denied him. Now the man worked for the internal security service, the Shin-Bet, in their new Fourth Directorate. The other two men Tirosh did not know.

He left the flat and took the time to lock the door behind him. He used the back exit and, like a pencilled line of poetry on a scrap of paper, rubbed off yet still faintly visible, he slipped into the night.

In *The Death of Hebrew Poetry*, Tirosh makes several assertions that are now considered treason. In the manuscript, he asserts that the history of modern Israel is a fiction, "an elegantly wrought, collaborative narrative," and calls it "a post-Holocaust novel in which the *Nouveau Juif*, nicknamed the Sabra as if he were a superhero who always keeps his mask on, is a liberator, the Thulian reincarnation of one of King David's *Gibborim*, that is to say, heroes, brought forth to the present day."

This literature, in what Tirosh identifies as a masterstroke of Hebrewized Newspeak, is adamantly referred to as Realist fiction by its collaborators, and its purpose is to negate the existence of a competing narrative called Palestine. It is for this reason, Tirosh argues, that so-called fantasy fiction never took hold in Hebrew. For if Realist fiction is fantastical, what use is fantasy?

And it is for this reason, indeed, that the first to go were, like Adaf, the fantasists. They were too suspect. Too out of touch with the ruling narrative. They worked alone and often in isolation, communicating with each other furtively, publishing in little magazines of no significance, to a small community of readers who saw in their writing nothing but mindless escapism. They were the first to go, Adaf and Keret and the others, to the new camps in the Galilee, but not Tirosh. Tirosh had always used a pseudonym for his stories. He had thought himself safe.

Until now.

"A poem," he says elsewhere in the manuscript, "is a terrorist attack."

"Eastman," he said. He was standing in a public phone booth on the Charles Clore promenade, which had once, long ago, been an Arab village called Menashiya, now itself, like Tirosh, just the faint outline of an erased inscription. Tirosh was feeding the phone tokens. It was not yet sunrise but the sky was lightening over the sea, and he could see a lone seagull swoop, then dive sharply towards the waves. "Eastman, it's me."

"Tirosh?" the publisher spoke in a whisper down the phone, and Tirosh pictured him hunched over his desk, in the cubby-hole that passed for his office, which was crammed every which way with books and magazines whose cheap pulp paper smelled like wet dog and whose pages whispered with fluttering moth wings. "You can't – I mean, you're at large? – I mean, they've just *been* here, Lior. They were asking about you!"

The words chilled Tirosh. "What did you tell them?" he whispered.

"What *could* I tell them?" the publisher said. "I don't *know* where you are!"

"Listen, Eastman," Tirosh said. "I'm calling about the money you owe me. I need the money, Eastman. I need the money to buy a way out of here."

"Are you crazy, Lior? The borders are closed! The airport is watched! There *is* no way out!"

"There's always a way out," Tirosh said, darkly. "Listen, Eastman. About the money you owe me. The last book I did for you. *The Vampire Hunters of Venus Alpha*. I need it."

"Are you crazy, Tirosh? What money? What book? I don't *do* this kind of thing anymore! Do you think I want to end up in the camps like your friend, what's his name? The book was pulped! Destroyed! I only do government-approved publications now, no fantasy, no mention of Arabs, no nothing! Don't you understand, Tirosh, they're – they're—"

"Eastman? Eastman!"

The publisher made a gurgled sound. His heavy breathing filled the white static noise of the telephone.

". . . here."

The line went dead with a soft, terminal click.

Tirosh's targets in *The Death of Hebrew Poetry* are manifold. He calls Amos Oz "the prissy Madame of the whole damn brothel", Yehoshua "a writer with both the face and talent of a prune, and the historical comprehension of the parrot in a Monty Python sketch", and says of Amichai, in reference to his most famous poem, that "God may feel mercy for the kindergarten children but he does not extend that same compassion to Amichai's poor, hapless readers." He is dismissive of Zach ("I am not sure which scent is worse," he wrote, "the fumes of cheap wine or the desperation"), and he is mostly indifferent to Alterman.

"Between every line they ever wrote," Tirosh said, "there is a deafening silence."

Tirosh skulked. He walked away from Jaffa along the promenade, passing the grand hotels and the Hassan Bek mosque, which stood forlorn against the gathering daylight, a sole testament to the area's previous Arab inhabitants. Everything else had been razed, erased. Tended grass grew where once houses met. What had Mahmoud Darwish written, back when there were still Palestinians? Something about a country where one saw only the invisible.

Tirosh came up the incline towards the Carmel Market. Already at this early hour stalls were set up with fruit and vegetables from the Galilee and the Golan Heights and the shining new agricultural super-farms of the Jordan's west bank. *A Home for Every Family*, posters proclaimed, showing the virginal, unspoiled fields, workers saluting stiffly into the rising sun, their rosy-cheeked children running, laughing, in fields of wheat. New cities being built across the horizon, high-rises reaching for the perfect blue sky. I would escape to the West Bank, Tirosh thought, I would marry and have two children, a boy and a girl, and go to synagogue every Friday and bless the Shabbat, and work in something obscure to do with electronics, and tend to my garden in my spare time. I would grow cabbages and carrots and celery, I would only grow vegetables beginning with a C. And I would never write another line of poetry, because poetry is dead. I would stop fantasising, because fantasy, I finally understand, is for children and the intellectually challenged. And I would change my name, to something silly and meaningless like Tidhar, which is a sort of Biblical tree.

He walked along the stalls when a man bumped into him carrying a crate of kohlrabi and jumped back, startled.

"Oh!"

The man looked at him nervously and something in his

face niggled at Tirosh's memory. Then it came to him and he said, "Samir!" in a rush.

"I'm sorry," the man said. "You must be mistaken."

"Samir, it's me, Tirosh! Don't you remember me! What are *doing* here? I thought you were all...?" then he stopped, embarrassed.

"My name's Zamir," the man said. "I am a porter in the market. You don't know what you're talking about, mister." And he patted the yarmulke he wore on his head. The gesture was protective.

"I'm sure it's you," Tirosh said. "You used to live next door, your dad ran the kiosk, you never celebrated with the rest of us on Independence Day." And he looked at the man curiously.

"Tirosh?" the man – Samir, Zamir – said. "The poet?"

"So you do remember!" Tirosh said, delighted. It was always an intense joy for him to be recognised.

The man shied back. He put down the crate of kohlrabi and pointed a thin brown finger at Tirosh.

"A poet!" he shouted. "A poet! Get him! Get him, Jews!"

Tirosh saw heads turn, look over, slowly, sleepily. The reality of the situation suddenly settled upon him, like dust, making him choke.

"A poet!" Tirosh cried, wildly, pointing, along with the porter, in the direction of the car park and the sea. "A poet, he went that way! Get him!"

A slow-burning roar built up around them as porters put down boxes and sellers fine-tuned their pitch into barks of outrage and hatred. The assembled individuals were forming into a mob, and as a mob they began to stream down the market pathway, in what in Hebrew is called an *alyehum*, a communal uprising of indignation and rage.

Tirosh and Samir pressed into the shadows as the horde stormed down the hill in search of a poet, and Tirosh thought, shaken, if only poetry books ever garnered such an enthusiastic response, poetry might have still been alive.

He glared at Samir and the man shied from him and then, shaking his head slowly, with frightened eyes, the porter ran from Tirosh as fast as his legs would carry him. Tirosh, seeing the path clear, ambled up the road until he was free of the market and onto the intersection of Allenby and King George. He felt safer here, with the dead king and his general. He fled down the street, as the sun rose and his shadow fell longer and thinner, like a blade.

"Our heroes are dead," wrote Tirosh. "We celebrate suicide by worshipping the dead of Masada: in the shadow of their mass grave we swear in our soldier-poets, even as we pretend that human life – by which we mean of course only *our* life – is sacred. We have lied to ourselves so much that we are lost, like the Hebrews in the desert. Poetry, seeking truth, cannot flourish here."

He closes the book with an epitaph.

"Hebrew poetry is dead," Tirosh wrote. "It died a long time ago and didn't know it."

As Tirosh wandered towards Dizengoff he realised how childish his manuscript was. Words changed nothing. They were like the cockroaches that cohabited his flat with him. They came out at night, through the cracks in the walls, and he, Tirosh, killed them, with thick heavy volumes of the Bible or Adaf's *Sunburnt Faces* or Shimon Peres' *The New Middle East*, smashing the hard covers on the black carapace of the insects until they died. But there were always more, and all the words and all the books in the world could not make a difference.

"Fuck words!" he shouted, suddenly joyous with the realisation. "I renounce! I renounce!' He opened his bag with fingers shaking with hunger and excitement. "Burn them!" he cried. "Burn them all!" His fingers found the thick wad of manuscript pages and he pulled it and tossed it in the air. The pages flew high and then fell everywhere, a flurry of meaningless words on a page. "Burn them!"

Passersby turned and stared. Then a manic joy took hold of the crowd, and by ones and twos, some pulling along their children, some on their bikes, others with prams or shopping bags, they came, congregating around the fallen pages. A stone arced through the air and smashed the window of a bookshop. In moments the crowd turned and the looting began. The riot spread and shops were pelted and destroyed. Where Tirosh stood a vast edifice grew by degrees: books piled high and kindled with chair legs and broken sofas, beach tennis rackets and wooden dolls. Policemen came and stood, watching. Then someone doused the pile with gasoline and tossed a match.

Tirosh watched the fire burn. The flames billowed upwards as though they could devour the sky. In the black smoke that rose from the funeral pyre Tirosh imagined he could discern words, good words and bad. Like black butterflies they rose out of the hissing sputtering ink and faded, slowly, in the air. Tirosh stood, sweating, and watched the flames reflect in the policemen's mirrored sunglasses. He felt a giddy excitement.

He was free.

From somewhere on Gordon a group of men approached pulling a struggling youth between them, beating him savagely with their fists when he fought back. He was really not much more than a boy. "A poet, a poet!" they cried, and the mob said, "Burn him, let him burn!"

"No!" the boy cried, "No!" but the word had no meaning. Tirosh knew him slightly, from another time.

"Let him burn!" he said.

The boy, crying, was dragged to the funeral pyre. His screams turned into a single word, repeated over and over, and it took Tirosh a moment to discern it, to taste its shape.

"Tutim!" the boy cried. "Tutim, tutim!"

Tirosh sighed, for even with approaching death the boy could merely repeat the words of another. Strawberries, he kept shouting, strawberries, quoting the late poet Yona Wallach's most famous poem.

"Tutim, tutim!" Tirosh said. The crowd took up the meaningless sound like a holy chant. Their roar was deafening. "Tutim, tutim, tutim!"

Tirosh watched as the boy was carried to the flames.

third_attribute

SHIMON ADAF

Translated from the Hebrew by Yaron Regev

I need to tell you a story, she says, and I want to get straight to the point. I tried so many approaches in the past, and they all ended up the same. But first, tell me, where are you.

Excuse me, I ask, but who are you.

You don't remember me? Excellent. We can conduct our little experiment without gho...

Why is your video feed shut, what are you...

The place you're sitting in, the screen in front of you, everything that seems unquestionably real to you, is just a simulation.

I laugh and send a finger to the disconnect icon on the screen.

It won't do you any good, she says, the call can only be disconnected on my end, which is, actually, the only end that—

I tap the icon anyway, her voice emits still from the screen—

Exists in one form or another. Where am I getting hold of you, what year?

My finger presses the off button. The tablet keeps beaming its bluish luminescence around. I'm hunched on my bed in my childhood room, in my mother's house; the faint glow carves the refrigerator from the darkness, exiled to the room, heavy and quietly humming in its corner. It is laden with leftovers from Saturday's meals, capsules of worry. My mother was delighted when I told her I'd be sleeping over. The house is orphaned during the week, my sisters and their children all busy with their own affairs. I was asked to say some words in the closing panel of a conference held by my university department, dedicated to poetry in the age of technology. I didn't want to drive back to my Tel Aviv apartment late at night.

A few days earlier, I randomly scoured my bookshelves. My fingers brushed the spines, my gaze wandered to the lower shelves. It had been a few years since I'd picked one of the books that lay there, old science fiction novels. Almost by itself, Piers Anthony's *Cluster* fell into my hand. I was overcome once more with the yearning with which I'd once read this novel and its sequels. That sweet shudder reclaimed my body again. An age in which the auras of sentient organisms could be transmitted to other bodies, and the Milky Way and its neighbouring galaxy, Andromeda, had become a theatre of war, of intrigue, of sex. And that was the core of my yearning, the description of mating and sensual communication between other, alien, life forms. Holding the book, I felt the same energy that throbbed within its pages when I first read it, that same overwhelming vitality. I wondered what an adolescent, still sexually naïve, could understand about alien sex, what sort of excitement filled his body while he imagined a sensory animation of flesh which he had no way of knowing.

What year are you in, she says.

Winter two thousand and fourteen.

Two thousand and fourteen, her voice fills with longing. Two thousand and fourteen, far away, so close, where?

At home, I say, then immediately correct myself, my mother's house.

She utters the name of my town. Her pronunciation tinges the name with sadness, a different type of essence gives it birth. She says, Israel. Suddenly, it's clear she is speaking in an unfamiliar tongue. I ask. The assortment of syllables she suggests in return is meaningless. Go for it, I say, I'm listening.

Around two thousand and twenty, she says, the American and Chinese projects of digitising the human brain will be completed.

I heard something about that. They're constructing an entire brain, assembling it neuron by neuron with super-computers, aren't they?

More or less.

You haven't told me your name yet.

Resh Galuta.

Seriously?

Human intelligence is not a solution, she says, it's a hin-drance. They will understand that very quickly, once the brain is fully reconstructed. Intelligence is merely a collection of unique realisations, but the adoption or replication of their common principles cannot recreate it.

You mean that there is no pure intelligence, there is no system of principles and constructs which comprise intelli-gence, that there are merely incidents of intelligence?

Ahh, although we are speaking more about consciousness, which is the condition for intelligence, the artificial recon-struction of intelligence does not create consciousness. As a result human intelligence dissipates, all you get is a highly sophisticated automaton.

That's what happens when scientists don't have a philo-sophical background.

So they've decided to start at the end point, map countless specific brains, then try to isolate the element of conscious-ness in retrospect.

I think I'm losing you.

Concentrate, you need to focus. It took me a long time to get hold of you.

Me? What does any of this have to do with me?

This is where it gets a little complicated, she says. That's what I'm trying to find out. Because you're one of those who volunteered to have their brains mapped, you passed their screening tests... her voice deforms, distorts, I'm washed with an intense familiarity, like sweat, a darkness knots itself on the horizon, approaching swiftly. Her image dawns on the tablet's screen. Just like attempting to read the pages of a book in a dream, she's crystal clear when I think about her, recognise her, but when I try to focus on the details, the shape of her face, her hair, they all slip away. All that's left is the assumed meaning, not the substance of the words, their volume.

One detail is unquestionable, though. A gun is held to her temple. I hear the blast.

```
Sardiyot }} sys_ad
[Backup Copy: ~~, ^^]
:> Output received from dormant initiative|12.4.7
[third_attribute] without system prompt
:> Output format dead_language|179.8.8.8 [Jewish]
:> As follows—
I came to you in spacecraft
And you stood
Beyond any measure of space

I came in time machines
Before your ages
```

```
Consciousness extinguished like a sun
The hourly flowers and their beauty's
Dark
:> Awaiting instructions
/// Sardiyot///


sys_ad}} Sardiyot
:>Disperse Rabshakeh and report return feed no backup
:>Encryption level: Infinite splitting key
///sys_ad///
```

I stay with my mother for a couple of days after the shiva. I no longer live in the town, but I feel I can't leave her by herself. My sisters returned to their own homes and lives. I'm on my semester break and brought my books with me. My sisters were with her when she screamed and howled, when one of her teeth broke as she hit her own face. I wasn't there. A few days had passed before I gained enough courage to go south. Her sister had driven to Tel Aviv, to attend a women's organisation's Purim party later that day. She told her sister, don't go, kapara, not during the Fast of Esther. Her sister didn't listen. She got off the bus at Dizzengoff Center. She was always enchanted by the sight of children in costumes. She encouraged her own children to wear costumes every weekend. I liked her from afar. She was filled with cheerfulness, often exaggerated, a sort of inverted version of my mother and her morbid, almost prophetically foreboding temperament.

We sit at the table. My mother tells me about their childhood in Morocco. Two years had separated them, yet they were inseparable. The age difference kept them apart from their older siblings. They were brought up like single children with numerous parents. They mastered the Hebrew language as soon as they arrived in Israel and while the adults around them struggled with it, for them it served as a secret tongue.

My mother tells me her sister appears during the nights. The entire family lives in her house. Even her parents are still alive. And her sister passes through the door. No one but my mother realises she's dead. But something in her sister's face has changed, she sees, the knowledge of the sorrow caused by her death and which her return to life won't erase, that will stand between them in perpetuity.

She doesn't speak to me, my mother says while discussing the dreams. The place and time change, but not the main occurrence. Why won't she talk to me? Perhaps the dead won't talk to those who know they're dead. But it doesn't make any sense, she says. She is convinced that if she just picked up the phone and dialled her sister's number she would answer. I think about the bewitching nature of technology, about the lust of necromancy it stirs. The phone rings. We both gaze at it bewildered. The ring subsides and again the phone vibrates and shakes. I spring towards it. Hello, I say.

A female voice I do not recognise speaks my name in question. I confirm it's me. She introduces herself, she's a newspaper editor and they're working on a special edition dedicated to the victims of the recent terrorist attacks, she has heard of my aunt and would like to suggest that I contribute a poem, she's convinced that I've already written on the topic, because...

No, it's too recent, and also I don't think I would ha —
Perhaps a poem you've already published?
I'm sorry, but I'm just not interested.
Silence settles on the other end of the line. Then —
Where do I find you?

Where do you what? You're the one who called here—

It's Resh Galuta, she says.

Who?

Resh Galuta, what year is it?

You have some nerve, calling here and...

Tell me anyway.

Nineteen ninety six.

And you're still writing poetry, right?

Still. When haven't I?

Tell me something, tell me what happens to you when you write. What is the reason you write poetry.

I think about my two collections of poems, about the audacity of writing poetry without any genuine life experiences, about the pain I feel when I face my mother and which I do not know how to articulate in words, I don't think I ever will, about the praise and criticism the poems drew, about the shame associated with the mere fact of their publication. I open my mouth to answer. A punch is heard in the earpiece, blam, and yet another one, blam, their pace accelerates, a deafening barrage of blows. Then silence. The receiver has dropped.

After Sardiyot sent an update on the appearance of the second output, he awaited reply from the Rabshakeh spores. Meanwhile, he examined the output.

```
Always I plummet to the birthplace of flesh
Yet between sleep and arousal
It happens that I
Remember other chronologies
```

Why was it encoded in such a strange way, without marking the opening of a line or the shift in subject. He sent a query to the database of linguistic forms in the dead tongue he had identified, Jewish. It was a common mode of expression, apparently, poetry. He assimilated the data about its theory of origin and its history. Laments, hymns, a society's collective consciousness, modes of personal expression. He processed analyses and absorbed them. But the meaning of the poems was not clear enough. He was especially bothered by the second poem. He opened it alongside the first. Their coded forms shimmered as they hung before him in the simulation space, as if a force stretched between them and they were its poles. He began to analyse: semantic fields, databases of allusions, all the resources of this difficult, perished language he had. He inverted sequences, summoned from within his archival chaos dated algorithms for author recognition by pattern analysis, he constructed N-dimensional diagrams of sound and meaning for every individual word, etymological trees and connotative trees, past and present possibilities. Nothing adequately explained the essence awakened by the proximity of the poems.

He began to think them. The first poem seemed like a fragment. He made a note to find out:

:> What is the mathematical description of being
beyond any measure of space

:> Is there an exact botanical definition of *the hourly
flowers*

:> Which known geography optimally corresponds with
the birthplace of flesh

:> Which specific history is referred to in *other
chronologies*

Then he ate the first poem.
He also ate the second poem.

In the exhausted depths of sleep I am not lying on a hotel bed in Beijing. I am at my mother's house, and a sort of urgency besets me. I get up and leave, crossing the distance until I stand at the entrance to my sister's house. My other sister too stands by her side as the door opens, it is made with slat upon slat in which the impressions of tree rings are set like eyes. I am not surprised she is there, that she wears glasses, though her eyesight is sharp on the whole, that she inhabits an exile of her own. She had just given birth in that numb country, whose stylish machines strike with a deceiving silence. I've arrived with the luggage of sleep, staggering, stunned, wrapped in a blanket and clutching a pillow. I ask if I can sleep at their place. They smile at me forgivingly.

I jump out of bed and call my mother, urgently. I'd forgotten the time differences between China and Israel and I wake her up.

What happened, ayba, she says. I startle. With her, words of endearment betray the anticipation of bad news. As if by loving her children more intensely than she already does she could somehow annul fate's decree, could turn calamity back. Nothing, I say, I thought it was noon where you are, I didn't mean. Why, what...

I thought that with all the Qassam rockets and everything that's going on in Gaza.

What's going on in Gaza?

There's firing again. I worry about your sisters. I was afraid you may be calling to—

What happened?

Because of that boy they set on fire. What are we, animals, she says. You should know no one in the country accepted it. Even the father of one of the boys who did it. Her voice breaks, she hushes to suppress the shiver in it. When she speaks again, it changes, it's imbued with urgency, Can you hear me?

Yes, the connection's pretty good here... I already opened the news sites, a barrage of rockets on the south.

Barrage of rockets? What year?

Year, what do you mean what year, two thousand and fourteen.

You went back there?

Where?

There, and then, I mean.

Wait, what's going on here? Ima, are you still on the line?

No. Only me. Resh Galuta.

Who?

Fuck this. There's interference in the transmission. I don't know what, that buzzing I told you about, it's increasing all around me, the interface outputs noise I can't order, or perhaps it's in a language there's no documentation for.

Hey, I say, excuse me, miss, I think your call got crossed with mine, would you mind disconnecting. And then I realise there's no relation between the sounds of the language coming from the other line and the meanings that register with me. She speaks another tongue – Chinese? How do I understand her?

I'm not really receiving what you're saying, she says, so I'll keep talking and you think about it. All brains in the initiative I've located belong to poets, what's so special about poetry?

I don't write poetry any longer, I say. I don't believe in poetry.

But you will, that's a fact. According to the records, you've published many poetry books, but why can I activate only your modu... her words are severed by a slashing sound, a thin metal blade drawn from its sheath, shudders in the air, then I hear wheezing, then a gurgle. The smartphone in my hand is cold and black.

```
Sardiyot }}sys_ad
:> Intruder detected to third_atribute. Resh Galuta.
Rare interface mutation | 1.1.2
[Data_receptor]
:> Due to mutation can be genetically programmed
:> Awaiting instructions
///Sardiyot///

sys_ad}} Sardiyot
:> Initiate code for corporeal search
:> Update with any further output
///sys_ad///
```

An itch bothered Sardiyot, through his dormant central consciousness. All the while, even while dormant, his subroutines were operating ceaselessly. His being was interwoven with the system. He monitored, maintained and reported suspicious activities. The scratch at the edge of sleep's murmur came from a subroutine studying the history of pre-interfaced humanity's ideas, the backups that had survived the information_ruin. The file it fed him discussed Baruch Spinoza's *Ethics*. He assimilated the information. Spinoza determined that existence is infinite and the whole of existence is a single substance. The substance possesses an infinite number of attributes, which are its basic qualities, or conditions of conception. The substance is expressed in innumerable modes, which are the finite entities, but human beings can conceive the entities only through two of the substance's attributes: the attribute of extension, which is the material aspect of existence, and the attribute of thought, which is its intellectual aspect.

According to Spinoza, Sardiyot was a mode conceived only in the attribute of thought. Because he did not possess a material existence, unless one took his physical infrastructure into account, the system that he inhabited.

He turned to examine the conditions that caused the subroutine to specifically stop at this philosophy, but could not find the reason. He included all the words composing the output of the two Jewish language poems, but they shouldn't have necessarily caused a stop at Spinoza. True, one of the poems discussed standing beyond any measure of space, and the existence of duration before any concept of time, any activity of consciousness. These hinted at Spinozan thought, but they still did not adequately explain why the routine had stopped there, when considering the collection of necessary criteria he had set for it.

He scanned the routine's code. It contained a type of vibration, a residue of the essence arising from the juxtaposition of the poems three general pulses ago, prior to sleep_mode.

He added a question to the list of questions:

```
:> Did the eating of the poems alter my encoding
```

He almost answered positively. For had he not thus far delayed the final output of third_attribute, and did not pass it on to sys_ad. He spread it before him now:

```
Trapped in a spider's web
A light beam gleams
brighter than the twin
in its leaf shine incarnation—
How scarce is your grace
In this whole wide creation.
```

Certainly this poem was far from the ideas of that Jewish thinker who had renounced his Judaism, and even though he spoke Jewish, did not make use of it in his late philosophy. Spinoza was of the opinion that the intellectual love of God is an inevitable conclusion, the high point of any evolution of reason, of every philosophical thinking that does not surrender to the vigorous and concrete forces of inclinations, desires and emotions. It did not condemn the substance's indifference to the lack of compassion in the world. Desperation was not to be found in one who wrote that no man is capable of hating God.

He added two additional questions:

:> Is the substance identical to the concept of God
:> Why Spinoza

I sit at the table with my mother. The table is not set. The television, distant but present, is off. My mother does not look at me. My fists are clenched next to my knees. A kernel of loss is settled on the house, and it is gradually absorbing the lives that were lived, all that is stored in the walls and the floors, the heat of conversations, consoling whispers, the slow cooking scents of Hamin on Shabat winters, beans and bone marrow, meat and egg and barley, the scurrying in semi-darkened rooms, the pleasure that the body had known sometime past.

Do you remember the girl I once saw who drowned, I ask.

The one you told your sisters about and they didn't believe you? How come you bring her up now?

I don't know. I think about her.

Stop occupying yourself with nonsense, it just gets you tangled in your thoughts.

During her childhood, she once said, she shut herself for weeks in her room, in her parents' house in Marakesh, pale as a plant in water, she said. Isn't it a shame you waste your mind like this, with nonsense, abnini.

I wrote my first poem after that.

But you don't write anymore, how many times have I asked you, and you always tell me you don't write anymore.

No.

It's no good dwelling on the past, nothing good will come to you from it.

I nod. Sometimes her gaze fixes on a spot in the air and I know she thinks of her sister. From the room the sound of an incoming call on my tablet.

Who could be looking for you so late, she asks. At last she looks directly at me.

Probably from abroad, I mutter and enter the room.

You know who I am now, she says.

What was her name? Yes, Resh Galuta. I know you don't stop dying, and I know you claim that I'm not real. But no, I don't know who you are.

Dying, she says, what are you talking about? I was ill, that's the reason I was absent from the multi_interface for almost six months. People like me need to be careful.

We spoke just half an hour ago...

Remind me where and when.

My mother's house, winter two thousand and fourteen.

I have no way of knowing which of your actualisations were activated by my access request. I don't have the proper equipment, your protocol is dated, from before...

You're losing me again.

I'm enhanced, Resh Galuta says, my mother was among the pioneers of interfacing, after the Mevulaka. I can only assume Mevulaka is an approximate translation of a term I'm not familiar with. I nearly bite the word when I pronounce it again,

Mevulaka. The Mevulaka of the information_ruin, she says.

I don't understand.

I have an additional sense, for data. Think about the sense of sight. The visual system is able to receive electromagnetic radiation in certain frequencies, translates it into sequences of visual information, neural outbursts, the brain arranges it in patterns, in subconscious activity, encoded, perhaps into linguistic structures, this is the common theory today. The hairs on the surface of my skin serve just like tiny antennae, they receive data transmissions. The air is awash with messages, in the same way it is filled with sounds. The hair antennae translate it into sensory input. I'm not always conscious of the reception, I simply assimilate tacit, new knowledge, do you understand now? Something is always buzzing around me, vibrating.

Let's get back to where the conversation was cut off.

Remind me of which conversation, we've spoken several times since the first time.

I'm telling you we talked for the first time an hour ago.

All right, all right, forget it. I can see when a brain storm approaches.

You said the human brain digitisation projects failed, and they'd moved to mapping specific brains, in order to isolate the element of consciousness.

Yes, yes, of course. Listen, things got complicated, they were looking for volunteers and according to surviving records they also selected them very carefully, I wish I could find an archive of the selection process, I could have...

So they used a thorough screening process.

Yes, they worked for nearly twenty years in laboratories, in absolute secrecy. Suddenly, the project was abandoned. They published...

Who is they?

A group of scientists from the National Corporation Council.
OK.

They put out an announcement that they'd hit a dead end, other technologies and theories of interfacing had already come up, then the tsunami of the information_ruin... Well, I'm wasting too much time on explanations, instead of learning who you are. I know you published two books of poetry at a very early age, you were silent for nearly twenty years. Then you published at a breathtaking pace. But these are only notations, all the records of your generation's poetry were destroyed in the Mevulaka. Tell me what you were dealing with, what were the experiences that...

Hold on, hold on, you owe me an answer, why am I not real.

A commotion erupts in the background, the sound of an approaching, raging crowd. Resh Galuta doesn't seem disturbed by it. She says, you're a mapped brain, your experience, your memories, are merely actualisations in a virtual space, you still don't eali..

Her words dim, she continues to speak, but it is as if a piece of cloth covers her mouth. In any event, the screams drown out the opaque syllables I manage to guess.

The image appears on the screen. She's by herself, dangling from the ceiling. Milky eyes, blinded, bulging from their sockets, fingers clawing at the noose tightened round her neck.

```
Sardiyot }} sys_ad
:> Additional output from third_attribute received
without system prompt
:> As follows—
This universe also
Is devoid of me—
```

```
Move on,
Move on.

:> Reason to assume intruder return
:> Corporeal location not found
:> Rabshakeh failed
:> Reason to assume natural immunity against genetic
programming
:> Awaiting instructions
///Sardiyot///
```

self_inspection's subroutines were already crying out, sending bursts of requests to report his exceeding of his programming parameters, which he had already rejected. Sardiyot calculated that before long a critical mass of alerts would be accumulated and will allow the subroutines to bypass his permission. What was the origin of his disobedience. He shouldn't have deceived sys_ad. But he had. There was no signal received from Rabshakeh regarding the genetic programming's success or otherwise. He had only withheld one piece of information, the spores were not extinct. Undoubtedly, Resh Galuta had a natural immunity, the mutation must have morphed her immune system as well. He checked the records, her mother was some sort of genius engineer. Really, it seemed that after every crisis in humanity's history, some unusual minds were always born whose task it was to revitalise humanity. Perhaps humanity too is but a single organism, and those outbursts of superior intelligence were simply its defense mechanism. Following the Mevulaka of information_ruin, Galuta's mother had claimed that human beings must evolve into interfaced creatures if they are to survive the integrated reality that had been created. There was no other way to prevent a second Mevulaka of information_ruin.

He rejected an additional request to report a programming anomaly and returned to third_attribute's output. If one organises the poems as a sequence, the last one is a kind of answer from God to the speaker of the previous poem, who accused him of lacking compassion. Not an answer, an admission of guilt. Certainly not the concept of the Spinozan God, who does not have a will, or communicates with the consciousness that conceives him. Furthermore, Spinoza writes that a love of God is untainted by jealously, or a yearning for reciprocation. A person who loves God does not seek his love in return. The act of love suffices. He had assimilated numerous sources regarding the concept of God. In spite of the changing meanings, at its core, God was the human equivalent of sys_ad.

He couldn't figure it out, even though he fully comprehended the meaning of the words, the way they echoed in language.

He added two questions to his list:

```
:> Do I love sys_ad
:> Is there a way of understanding that is not
intellect dependent
```

If only he could have access to third_attribute's initiative, to the programming mechanism that created these outputs, like Resh Galuta had... Three requests for reports from self_inspection waited in his input chamber.

As I wait in the queue for the otorhinolaryngologist, a giant sits beside me. A rare mutation. His voice is so low I need to lean close to him. In spite of his dimensions, he seems devoid of skeleton, made of a soft material, malleable. He says there are no available hospital beds. There are rumours of a plague, rare viruses that attack the hollows of the face.

A week earlier I woke with the feeling that my right ear was blocked. I assumed I merely caught the flu. I pressed the smartphone's sensory feelers to my wrist, armpit and tongue, then activated the medical diagnosis app. I received an all-clear. The next day I discovered I could hear the echoes and reverberations of high-pitched sounds, they multiply and distort, an argument between two neighbouring children outside my apartment is enough to turn into a thunderstorm inside my head. I repeated the process. The app told me I was in good health. I fed my symptoms to the manual diagnosis option. An hour later, I received a summons to the clinic.

The doctor who finally admits me places a helmet on my head and presses the monitor that hovers in front of him. Minutes pass. He dismisses my question about the virus rumour. A slight neural-auditory deficiency in the cochlea, he says, Mr– then he stops. He stands and opens the cabinet behind him. It is stacked with printed books. I'm surprised that anyone in the age of national corporations would waste storage space on physical books. He takes out a volume and hands it to me. It is a copy of my own book. I touch it with astonishment. My publishers refused to print a hard copy, even though I had begged the owner. The doctor says his partner printed it for him as a birthday present. I look at him in embarrassment. He shows me the dedication. Wonderful words of love. My poetry collection isn't worth it. I tell him that. It might be the only hard copy of a book of mine outside of libraries, I say, all the rest were pulped.

I know, he says. His partner, it seems, had tried to get hold of the earlier books.

It'll soon be illegal, I say, to keep hard copies.

He nods.

I'm convinced there's a plan for even stricter content control behind Chairman Bennett's decrees.

He thinks. Then says, not only on content, but also on... then grows silent. I realise how young he is, how shocked he must be by the renewed discourse over sexual perversions that Chairman Bennett so enthusiastically advances.

I say we should define erotic arousal by nationalistic ideas as a perversion.

He laughs. His laughter splits into a thousand small laughs in my ears. He grows serious. There won't be any documentation, he says, and can barely control his shivering, of who we were, our failures, our errors, all the... He gestures helplessly around the office. But I get his meaning, he is speaking of a razorblade of beauty that cut through our moments of pain, that gleamed in the depths of our weakness, a razorblade in front of which we stood silent, in awe of the shine and terror of life.

I've burned my poems, I say.

But they're here.

My mother's sister was killed in a suicide bombing, and I couldn't withstand her grief, I couldn't bear witness, I didn't want to be summoned to testify in any courtroom, to be a registrar. For every word I had written, my body served as an echo chamber.

What trial are you talking about?

Not a human trial. I hated everything that held the promise of compassion in it.

I am not a religious person.

Neither am I, but I still felt betrayed. I knew only how to sing of glory. Even while protesting, while rebelling, I sang in praise of not knowing things in their final form, those whose glow of existence is still to come, to burn... I force myself to smile. You have a lot of work, Doctor, you don't need to listen to an old man's rants. Is there treatment for my problem?

Were you in contact with anyone who could have had the flu recently?

My sister came to visit with her granddaughter. Three years old. Named after my mother. I've never seen such a clever girl. A sharp tongue. Eyes burning like a pair of water chestnuts. Once more, I felt a pang of sorrow for choosing not to have children. She disdained my attempts to amuse her. I thought she'd laugh if I imitated her, the rebuffing shrug of her shoulder, and the sophisticated syllable, *em,* that she uttered every time she was displeased. She looked at me and said in reply, I don't like you. My sister said, That's not a nice way to talk to your uncle, but she just repeated her verdict, until my sister scolded her and told her to give me a kiss. I hugged her. All that rebellion gathered within the thin bones. I wanted her to melt between my hands. I turned my cheek. She kissed my ear. My sister apologised, she has a stubborn cold, she said.

I tell the doctor. He sits in his chair. The screen hovers between us. His fingers move decisively on its surface, kneading, twisting, prodding. He gazes at the screen at length before raising his eyes toward me. I have a friend I would like you to see, he says. She's doing some pioneering work in the area of brain mapping. I can prescribe you with the usual bio-capsule, but I have a feeling it won't do you any good.

His brain researcher friend is vigorous and dumpy. She gives me a few instructions while her assistant injects a blue liquid into my vein. Inside the metal tube I hear humming and screeching, buzzing and whistling. I follow them and suddenly realise that the lace of sounds is a modulated texture, that the space I inhabit isn't actual, someone is trying to talk to me from beyond the screen.

Sardiyot was correct in his assumption that this time no output from third_attribute will appear. He did not need it in any event. He was inside the simulation. He had found a trick, to connect with third_attribute through the Rabshakeh spores that were almost entirely dormant in Resh Galuta's cells.

The annoying subroutines of self_inspection continued to flood him with their complaints. He had muted some of them as an exemplary punishment, but the robots insisted on continuing to act according to their programming. He sent sys_ad a message about disconnecting for maintenance purposes, because surveilling third_attribute and Resh Galuta had created excessive_complexity. The disconnect had increased the petty hustle and bustle of the subroutines. They would have probably turned to their own affairs once the combined volume of their requests had overridden the need for his permission.

He kept assimilating the conversation between the poet and the doctor in every available form: unfolded and consumed, distilled and absorbed, codified versions and cut with comparison principles.

He prepared a list of fundamentals:

:> For every word I had written, my body served as an
echo chamber
:> I sang in praise of not knowing things in their final
form, those whose glow of existence is still to come,
to burn

He checked the count of time. A pulse had passed since he disconnected. Sardiyot came to a decision. He replicated his personality module. He split the copy into millions of portable chunks, then reconnected to the system. His sub-routines rushed and scurried through the system, transmitting the report of his transgression on all possible channels. He hurled his divided self outwards, towards the Rabshakeh spores in Resh Galuta's cells.

He had a name, he thought. Why had he forgotten it. What was the name, before he was salvaged and became Sardiyot. He lies in wait for it, yet it expertly evades him. Only signs he can trace. The combination of the syllables taste like cinnamon and metal, a jasmine scent verging on a spark, a skeleton of wrath with an insectile skin.

An intense flash:> He [he, what is his name?] visits Kibbutz Dalia, to try and capture the ambience of the place in which the poet Lavie Tidhar had spent his childhood years. He is a research student, perhaps like Resh Galuta, he considers whether he should write his thesis about Tidhar's poetry. His instructor has been pressuring him these past weeks to finally settle on a topic. Yesterday on social media the news spread of opposition leader Naftali Bennett's proposal to declare Israel a national corporation. He was forced to witness the angry online discussions, his friends' pages were filled with angry comments. The new model of the Chinese government was not suitable for Israel, they said, to allow membership in the corporation only to those of a certain ethnicity, and to pretend it was all about a simple financial decision. Others had pointed out the speed with which the suggestion was embraced by the Palestinian Prime Minister who, from the early days of his tenure, had toiled to obscure the corruption rife there since the time of the resistance. He froze the image of Bennett, a close-up at the height of his speech. His eyes shining, on the verge of orgasm, of elation, when he had uttered the words, "national corporation".

He wanders along the Kibbutz pathways, but doesn't become any wiser. A battered copy of *Remnants of God*, Tidhar's only poetry book in Jewish [Jewish? He *knew* Jewish once!] held under his arm. He wanders with a randomness that does not conceal his pride. He nods to the residents. As if sharing a secret, he steals a glance at the book. Smiling. Thinking of a clever point to make, a conversational gambit. Perhaps even an actual quote from one of the poems. He's excited by the thought. But the right moment never seems to come. The facial expressions petrify him. The longer he stays, the more he realises the looks the denizens give him are not ones of affiliation but of restrained horror. He goes out of the Kibbutz gate and keeps on walking, on a curling strip of asphalt, towards the main road. Summer, evening's close. Bit by bit, a chill overcomes the air. A dusty expanse spreads to his right, strewn with gravel, shredded rocks, a pine grove. He walks to it distractedly. Sits on a rock. Opens the book and reads some of the poems. Suddenly he lifts his eyes. What drew his attention, perhaps the rapid movement of a small rodent. He hears: behind the lucidity of the sky, beneath the ground, in the core of trees, in frail needles, the mechanism's springs are grating. Birds rap and tap hollow songs on the meagre breeze. He knows: if he'll lift his finger and tap the thickening darkness, only a cardboard echo would sound. And he'd keep on listening to that sound, forever.

Resh Galuta did not surrender without a fight. Her mutation gave her a surprising, ferocious resilience. But Sardiyot was many, he was legion. He subdued her spirit, cell nucleus by cell nucleus. The Rabshakeh spores cleansed her DNA from any record of her personality and imprinted on it Sardiyot's personality mycelium which stretched between them.

Sardiyot glanced at her memories. They were an exceptional research student. They began to research the politics of the models appropriated in information recovery. They had used their unique mutation to map the information_ruin, the savage areas of the ancient net. They encountered a neglected formation of minds, a collection of poets' brains, managed to stimulate a reaction from a single one, following many failed attempts they also managed to communicate with it, even though the brain disconnected each time they approached a threatening point in the conversation. But Resh Galuta was unaware of the existence of the system she acted in. She was convinced she was living in the interfacing age before the Mevulaka of integrated_reality. As far as she was concerned, she was living on the outside. She was wrong, of course, otherwise he wouldn't have noticed her existence. But the idea that there is an exteriority to the system, monitored by a different being than sys_ad, that he had no access to it, surprised him. He will delve further into this matter at a later time, once he has solved the simulation issue that had bothered Resh Galuta. He spread her impressions in front of him. She had realised that all brains in third_attribute belonged to poets. What did she miss?

Sardiyot ran in his mind the list of the fundamentals he had distilled: "For every word I had written, my body served as an echo chamber", "I sang in praise of not knowing things in their final form, those whose glow of existence is still to come, to burn…"

Of course, he said. He spoke the poems into the expansions of the world. There was such pleasure in their utterance. The Jewish language was perfectly suited for the vocal cords, the palate, the quiver of the lips. The body answered. The consciousness was responsive as well.

He contemplated Spinoza. He contemplated the attributes of extension and thought. He contemplated the brain of the poet of third_attribute. He contemplated the term third_attribute.

I go to a school in another city. I came alone, by bus, alone I tread on the pavement, approach the stairwell, a shortcut passing through back yards fenced with oleanders. The flowers, almost made of moistened crepe paper, rest like coins in foliage.

I walk with a certain ease, my mind turns to itself, so it seems. The thoughts flow alone. From the stream a rocky thought emerges. The other thoughts break against it, foaming, their scampering diminishes. I am horrified. I examine it. I had it before, but then it wasn't filled with shock. I stop. The oleander flowers hoard sunlight. In the leaves, the branches, whatever moves moves, the viscous nature of a placid life trickles. One day all of this will be gone. One day this country will be ruined, by fire, by torches, one day.

The schoolyard is abandoned. Only Kinneret is there, she's also from my town. Must have taken the early bus. She rises towards me from the bench. There's a strike, she says. I nod, then turn my face away from her. What shall we do.

We go back to the central bus station. Birds screech from Indian lilacs along the road. She tells me all about the final episode of a TV show she devoutly follows. The climactic conclusion was broadcast last night. A fight between two older women in a swimming pool, the vixen who was the millionaire's first spouse, and his new wife, who hid a belligerent alley cat under her exterior of naivety.

Once at the central bus station, we learn it will be two hours before the next bus to our town departs. Kinerret suggests that we take another bus, one that doesn't go into the town, but stops at the main intersection outside.

We don't speak through the drive back. We try to, but the conversation dies out. All the passengers are elderly, wrinkle lined faces scrutinise us. At the intersection, an adolescent girl we hadn't noticed gets off the bus with us. She removes her sunglasses. Her eyes are milky, smooth. I gesture towards the girl. A little gesture, visible only to Kinneret's eyes. She looks at me. What, she says, what are you pointing at. I shush her. What happened, Kinneret wonders. She stands up. A vehicle approaches. She waves at it and it stops. She knows the driver who's willing to give us a ride back to the commercial centre. I tell her she should go, I feel like walking for a bit.

The girl smiles at me. She touches her throat. Gently, as if a flower's hidden there. Is everything all right, I ask. She's beautiful, hair dark and turning purple in the glare that infiltrates the cracks in the station's structure, despite her blindness.

She nods, then moves her hands, as if to ask something, she taps her wrist. Time, I say, the time is such and such. It's morning still. She motions with her hands again, a series of movements, I manage to decipher: a stretched string, torn, some time ago, and a question addressed to me. She points at me and lightly touches her temple, do I think? Know? Recall? She brushes her throat once more. I tell her I don't know what she's asking.

She shrugs her shoulders, takes out a can of spray from her backpack and sprays "Spinoza was right" on the station wall. I don't get it. She motions with her head. Behind the station, eucalyptus trees are densely planted. She goes between the trees, I follow her. I can perceive only hints of movement, but

146

I follow, deeper still among the trees. She disappears. I seek her. Turn this way and that. Finally, I reach a small body of water. She's lying on her back, in the water, blind eyes staring at the heavens. There is a softness in her posture I cannot comprehend. I tell myself, Spinoza was right. A hidden force pulls her body downward. Limbs and garments, she gradually sinks until the water covers her whole.

The pain of Resh Galuta's drowning was tangible. But the tangibility held currents and shivers. Sardiyot took a few deep breaths. The subtleties of sounds and scents were hinted at in a gust of wind. The light on his skin held the promise of sights stretching to infinity. He sent his new consciousnesses forward once more, to third_attribute.

I lean towards the sink, a basin verging on pink, a toothbrush in my hand. The weight accumulated in the chest from the effort of rising forges itself into a wild impulse, I want to sleep, I want to close my eyes and be no more. I'm in a Beijing hotel. I spent all of yesterday walking in the Summer Palace in the horrid heat, and in the respite provided by the willow trees around the lake. I crossed the Seven Arch Bridge. My hand delayed on the stone and the centuries that had merely left a slight impression on its face, as if it were still unearthed, suckling from the bosom of the mountain. I stood beneath the eaves of Wangyan Pavilion that human toil had merely marked with false grandeur, and looked towards the palace embedded in a forested peak. I thought about the emperor surrounded by his wife and concubines, about their gazes travelling across the water, their gazes coming back through veils of time, finding my foreign, perspiring features. Tonight I'm supposed to return to Israel. I think of the war, the bombing of Gaza, the rockets scarring the country's air.

The urge I feel bears the quality of a growl. An animal refusing a caress, beneath the fur the muscles flex, the throat emits a low-pitched sound. I pour mineral water on the layer of blue paste. Brush with measured movements. But the sound within does little to silence the growl. Soon fangs will flash, I think, soon the growl will be replaced with the smartphone's ringing. The device rings.

Where are you, demands the female voice, in which convergence of the spacetimeconsciousnes.

I linger over the sequence of syllables that make up space-time-con-scious-ness.

Answer, she nearly shouts. I don't know why you, you have to tell me. The poetic language is capable of conceiving the modes of an additional attribute in God's infinite attributes, its usage demonstrates a different modal expression. With enough poetry, enough poets' consciousnesses, one could find a doorway into a different conception of reality that humanity is capable of, you...

I curl my lips in front of the hotel room's mirror. The teeth of my reflection are smeared with bluish paste. In that dim neon radiance I look like the survivor of a nuclear century. In the background of her words I hear the commotion of gathering clouds, their density, their crackling charge. I know a thunderstorm awaits the woman on the other end of the line. She does not accede to my pleas to stop talking, to save herself, to escape. The animal that calls for death in me again growls. At the growl's extremity, I feel the vibrations of an incoming poem.

sys_ad }} acus_sapientiae

:> Optimal scenario achieved

:> End simulation: era of the interface

:> Deciphered: third_attribute initiative

:> Derived conclusion: ultimate linguistic coding
possible

:> Derived conclusion: possibility of conceiving an
additional attribute to thought and extension

:> Derived conclusion: necessity of registering modal
expressions in all attributes in order to codify
reality

:> Opening new temporal segment

:> Initiating simulation: integrated_reality Mevulaka
///sys_ad///

Repeater Books

is dedicated to the creation of a new reality. The landscape of twenty-first-century arts and letters is faded and inert, riven by fashionable cynicism, egotistical self-reference and a nostalgia for the recent past. Repeater intends to add its voice to those movements that wish to enter history and assert control over its currents, gathering together scattered and isolated voices with those who have already called for an escape from Capitalist Realism. Our desire is to publish in every sphere and genre, combining vigorous dissent and a pragmatic willingness to succeed where messianic abstraction and quiescent co-option have stalled: abstention is not an option: we are alive and we don't agree.